Contents

First and foremost this book is dedicated to the memory of the innocent civilians, particularly the children, who suffered and died during the siege. Secondly to Dorothy (my mum), Angie the ever patient and to Charlotte, Alex and James my children, who, thankfully, have never had to experience the suffering described in these pages. A final dedication goes to the members of the Belanovsky family who were there.

IMAGES OF WAR
LENINGRAD
HERO CITY

RARE PHOTOGRAPHS FROM WARTIME ARCHIVES

NIK CORNISH

Pen & Sword
MILITARY

First published in Great Britain in 2011 by
PEN & SWORD MILITARY
an imprint of
Pen & Sword Books Ltd
47 Church Street
Barnsley
South Yorkshire
S70 2AS

ISBN 978 1 84884 514 5

A CIP catalogue record for this book is available from the British Library

Typeset in Gill Sans by
Phoenix Typesetting, Auldgirth, Dumfriesshire

Printed and bound in England by
CPI UK

Pen & Sword Books Ltd incorporates the Imprints of Pen & Sword Aviation, Pen & Sword Family History, Pen & Sword Maritime, Pen & Sword Military, Pen & Sword Discovery, Wharncliffe Local History, Wharncliffe True Crime, Wharncliffe Transport, Pen & Sword Select, Pen & Sword Military Classics, Leo Cooper, The Praetorian Press, Remember When, Seaforth Publishing and Frontline Publishing

For a complete list of Pen & Sword titles please contact
PEN & SWORD BOOKS LIMITED
47 Church Street, Barnsley, South Yorkshire, S70 2AS, England
E-mail: enquiries@pen-and-sword.co.uk
Website: www.pen-and-sword.co.uk

Preface

The siege of Leningrad is one of the epic operations of the Second World War on the Eastern Front. During the 900 days that the siege officially lasted the suffering endured by the garrison and civilians within the, as the Soviets termed it, Blockaded area was almost unimaginable, particularly during the first winter.

The city of Leningrad formerly, and once again, St Petersburg was the capital of Russia from 1732 to 1918, when an earlier German offensive threatened the survival of the fledgling Soviet state and necessitated the transfer of the seat of government to Moscow.

It was Lenin's Bolshevik Party that, in November 1917, ousted the original revolutionaries of March 1917 in the city of Petrograd, as St Petersburg became in 1914, to distance it from German connections, to create the birth place of the Soviet state. It was this symbolism, coupled with the city's industrial capacity – including two tank factories and several naval yards, and strategic significance – its proximity to Finland, and its importance as a transport hub that drew it to Hitler's attention during the planning stages of Operation Barbarossa.

Within the confines of such a book as this it is almost impossible to do justice to the scale of the siege. Therefore, what it is intended to do is provide the general reader of military history with a heavily illustrated overview of the campaign. There are more scholarly books, such as Harrison Salisbury's *900 Days: The Siege of Leningrad*, on this topic and these are commended to the reader who wishes to learn more.

St Isaac's Cathedral silhouetted against machine-gun fire. (From the fonds of the RGAKFD at Krasnogorsk via Nik Cornish)

Introduction

The city that became Leningrad was founded as a result of war and the ambition of Tsar Peter (the Great) to modernize his empire in 1703. It was established on the site of a former Swedish fortress at the mouth of the Neva River. By the late eighteenth century the city had expanded, although at great human cost – thousands of conscripted serfs died during the years of construction carving out building plots from the marshy forests, to become the pre-eminent city of Russia.

As the imperial capital it was only natural that revolutionaries of all persuasions should gravitate towards it and the nineteenth century witnessed a burgeoning of anti-tsarist movements. However, it was the reign of Tsar Nikolas II that was finally to witness the trio of revolutions that swept the Romanov dynasty from power. Although marginalized, the revolutionaries watched and waited until, at the height of the First World War, during March 1917 the opportunity they dreamt of presented itself. Within a week the Tsar had abdicated and was replaced with a more liberal regime named the Provisional Government. However, the Provisional Government had from the outset a rival to its power namely the Petrograd Soviet, which became the body through which Lenin's Bolshevik Party stormed to power in November 1917.

With the Russian army demobilizing and the threat of a German march on the city, Lenin transferred the government to Moscow during the summer of 1918. Although threatened with capture by the anti-Bolshevik army of General Yudenitch in 1919 and the uprising of the naval garrison at Kronstadt during 1921, the city remained firmly Bolshevik and was rewarded following the death of Lenin in 1924 by being renamed Leningrad.

This coincided with the creation of the Leningrad Military District (LMD), the premier military district of the Soviet Union. In the event of war the LMD would form Northern Front, which roughly equated with a German army group. Consequently, its responsibilities included the mobilization of air, sea and ground assets as ordered by the General Staff and the People's Commissariat for Defence (NKO).

For the next decade the LMD was at the forefront of military developments, including theories of airborne assault and deep-penetration operations as outlined by the ill-fated Marshal M. N. Tukhachevsky.

When the Soviet Union went to war with Finland in November 1939 the conduct of the responsible military district, Leningrad, was appalling. The men were ill equipped, the tactics abysmal and the approach apathetic. Therefore, it was superseded by North Western Front which was disbanded at the war's end in March 1940. Shamed from its torpor by the Russo-Finnish War the Red Army strove to modernize its forces, theories and weaponry.

However, when the Baltic States were incorporated into the Soviet Union, during the spring of 1940, a new military district was created named the Baltic Special Military District (BSMD), which was in the event of war to become North Western Front. North Western Front was tasked with defending the Baltic States and therefore the western approaches to Leningrad. The LMD now became responsible for not only the territory of the Leningrad *oblast* (district) but the border with Finland from the Arctic Circle and the Estonian coastline. To fulfil this part of the Soviet Defence Plan for 1941 Fourteenth Army would cover the frontier from Murmansk to Lake Onega, Seventh Army the gap between lakes Onega and Ladoga and Twenty-Third Army the Karelian Isthmus land bridge to Leningrad. Consequently, in June 1941 almost all of LMD's forces were facing the Finns. The NKO's confidence in North Western Front covering Leningrad's flank was, however, sadly misplaced as events were to show.

On 22 June 1941, when the Germans unleashed Operation Barbarossa, the commander of the LMD was Lieutenant General M. M. Popov. So concerned was he about the reliability of North Western Front's abilities to protect his flank that he ordered an inspection of the district's southern and western defences. The resulting report recommended the construction of a defensive line along the course of the Luga River from Narva to Lake Ilmen.

Facing each other on the approaches to Leningrad were Germany's Army Group North (AGN), commanded by Field Marshal Ritter von Leeb, and the BSMD, commanded by Colonel General F. I. Kuznetsov. On paper both were powerful forces: however, there the similarity ended. AGN's Sixteenth and Eighteenth armies along with Fourth Panzer Group were experienced campaigners with the clear brief to overrun the Baltic States. Then, with the support of Army Group Centre, Kronstadt the home of the Red Banner Baltic Fleet and Leningrad would be taken. Following the successful conclusion of this plan, 'we initiate operations to seize Moscow'.

Kuznetsov's orders were less clear. Under strict instructions to avoid provoking the Germans during the early hours of Barbarossa, he effectively lost the initiative as North Western Front was penetrated in some places up to a depth of 80km. The front's three armies, Eighth, Eleventh and Twenty-Seventh, were, by early July, in complete disarray. Supply and communications systems had almost disintegrated, tactics were shown to be outmoded and air cover was disorganized. The defence line of the Dvina River had been broken, which resulted in Kuznetsov's replacement by Lieutenant General P. P. Sobenikov, but the real power was in the hands of the new chief of staff Lieutenant General N. F. Vatutin, who was ordered to restore some semblance of order to North Western Front.

None of this critical situation was overlooked by Popov or the leader of the Leningrad Communist Party, A. A. Zhdanov, a hard-line supporter of Stalin. On 4 July the Red Army's Chief of Staff, General G. K. Zhukov, instructed Popov's Northern Front to 'immediately occupy a defence line along the Narva–Luga–Staraia Russia–Borovichi front'. Popov created the Luga Operational Group (LOG) to carry out this task. The battle for Leningrad's outermost line of defence was about to begin.

The old regime, with Tsar Nikolas II at the extreme left of the photograph, participating in the ceremony of the Blessing of the Waters. The flags of the Guards are blessed in St Petersburg in commemoration of Christ's baptism. As the depot for the Guard's cavalry and infantry corps the city was the most important military district in the country. (Courtesy of the Central Museum of the Armed Forces Moscow via Nik Cornish)

The new, Bolshevik, regime in the persons of a shore party from the Baltic Sea Fleet. Seen here checking the credentials of a civilian driver, the Baltic Fleet's sailors were amongst the most committed supporters of the Bolshevik revolution. However, when disillusion set in during 1920–1 their protests were ferociously crushed. Nevertheless, with its shipyards and the proximity of the fleet Leningrad remained an important naval base. (Courtesy of the Central Museum of the Armed Forces Moscow via Nik Cornish)

Officers of the Red Army pose for the camera during the summer manoeuvres carried out by the Leningrad Military District between the wars. During this period the commanders of the LMD included Marshal Tukhachevsky, a pioneer military theorist who fell foul of Stalin and was purged, as well as Marshal Shaposhnikov, one of Tukhachevsky's betrayers. (Nik Cornish at Stavka)

The LMD was responsible for the early period of the Russo-Finnish War, which raged from November 1939 until March 1940. The poor performance of the Red Army during this conflict encouraged Hitler's ambition to eradicate the USSR. Here a Soviet machine-gun crew advances across snowy terrain with men and weapon on skis. (From the fonds of the RGAKFD at Krasnogorsk via Nik Cornish)

Having concluded the Finnish conflict the USSR further extended its borders by absorbing the Baltic States of Estonia, Latvia and Lithuania following an ultimatum and a march through the region by Soviet cavalry from the Leningrad Military District in mid-June 1940. Estonian cavalrymen such as those seen here put up no resistance. (Nik Cornish at Stavka)

As the USSR recovered from the Finnish conflict and absorbed the Baltic States the Germans overran Western Europe in a series of campaigns that blooded their forces and proved the efficacy of Blitzkrieg tactics. These German soldiers are manhandling a 37mm anti-tank gun across a French stream. It would prove a less-effective weapon against Soviet armour. (Nik Cornish at Stavka)

Chapter One

A Time of Great Peril

In reality Zhukov's order to Popov had simply confirmed actions that were already underway. Work had by this time begun on the Luga Line which was to form the first barrier between AGN and Leningrad. A second line some 21–9km out from the city was also being planned. This would run from Peterhof, through Krasnogvardeisk to Kolpino. This in turn was supported by a third line which utilized the railway line from Avtovo to Rybatskoe on the Neva River.

To coordinate the activities of Northern and North Western fronts Stalin appointed Marshal K. E. Voroshilov as their overall commander on 10 July. Voroshilov was an old friend of Stalin's from the revolutionary and civil-war days but poorly suited to the demands of modern warfare. Three days after his appointment Voroshilov announced that Leningrad would be held 'at all costs'. Unfortunately, that same day elements of the Fourth Panzer Group crossed the Luga River and established several bridgeheads. However, these footholds were not expanded due to the firm resistance of 2nd DNO (the Soviet acronym for People's Militia Divisions), stiffened with two companies of officer cadets and the panzers lack of infantry support. Leningrad was now less than 115km away.

To the south 8th Panzer Division was acting as the advance guard of the push to Novgorod and beyond that aimed at cutting the Moscow–Leningrad railway line at Chudovo. However, Vatutin launched a counter attack at Soltsy, isolated 8th Panzer Division and reduced its armoured strength by some 50 per cent; it also gained precious time for the teams of workers labouring on the defence lines. Von Leeb decided to call a halt to the advance in order to enable AGN's supply echelons to catch up and to improve the security of AGN's rear areas, which were awash with Red Army stragglers who posed a continual threat to communications and resupply.

Finland had begun what they termed the 'Continuation War' with an offensive to regain the land lost during the Winter War of 1939–40. The Finns pushed back Twenty-Third Army, which was reinforced with two divisions from northern Karelia. Another two divisions from the same source went to bolster the line in Estonia where AGN's Eighteenth Army was making steady progress. The recently formed Soviet High Command, the Stavka, now began to reinforce North Western Front. The five infantry and two cavalry divisions of Thirty-Fourth Army were followed by the newly formed Forty-Eighth Army.

Both were to take up positions south of Lake Ilmen to protect Northern Front's left flank. By early August Voroshilov's ineptitude was becoming more apparent and Stalin berated him for his weakness in leading North Western Front in particular. On 8 August Eighteenth Army reached the Gulf of Finland, an event that coincided with Hitler's announcement that AGN would be reinforced by XXXIX Motorized Corps, a powerful force of two motorized and one panzer division, as well as Fliegerkorps VIII, the Luftwaffe's strongest ground support unit on the Eastern Front.

Von Leeb created three groups to undertake the conquest of Leningrad: the Northern Force to press from Narva in Estonia to Kingisepp, a vital road and rail junction to the east and less than 160km from Leningrad; it included XLI Motorized and XXXVIII army corps. The Luga Group in the centre was to strike Leningrad through the town of Luga and included LVI Motorized Corps plus 8th Panzer Division. General Erich von Manstein's LVI Motorized Corps also had orders to meet the Finns east of Lake Ladoga on the Svir River, which if he succeeded would cut Leningrad off from the rest of the Soviet Union other than by air. The Southern Group of I and XXVIII army corps would advance to the south of Leningrad, cutting the land links to Moscow and join up with the Finns. Sixteenth Army's II and X army corps would take Staraia Russia, Velkie Luki and move into the Valdai Hills. Finally, two infantry divisions of Eighteenth Army's XXVI Corps would push along the Estonian coast to Tallinn depriving the Baltic Fleet of its last base before Kronstadt itself.

In Moscow Stavka was aware of the German preparations and ordered Voroshilov to launch a pre-emptive attack in the Dno-Soltsy area on 12 August. Four of North Western Front's armies, Eleventh, Twenty-Seventh, Thirty-Fourth and Forty-Eighth, would undertake a pincer movement to encircle X Army Corps. The plan almost came unstuck as von Leeb moved first, striking with Manstein's corps. Nevertheless, Vatutin's attack also went ahead and rapidly cut off X Army Corps and penetrated 25km westwards, threatening the rear of the units heading for Novgorod. Shuffling his forces rapidly, von Leeb, by weakening his strike groups, first contained then drove back the Soviets. Although Vatutin had not achieved his objective, he had disrupted his opponent's plans but it was temporary. Between 8 and 21 August the Soviets defending the Kingisepp sector were, despite valiant efforts, driven back.

By 1 September all that remained of North Western Front's Eighth Army was penned into a marshy enclave around Oranienbaum on the Baltic coast.

AGN's Luga Group, having held Vatutin's attack, took Luga itself on 24 August. Novgorod had fallen to the Southern Group eight days earlier, followed by Chudovo on 20 August. Aware that Vatutin's efforts had been marginalized, Stavka reorganized. Northern Front was split into the Karelian and Leningrad fronts under Lieutenant General V. A. Frolov and Popov respectively. Popov's command included the Baltic Fleet (commanded by Admiral V. F. Tributs), Eighth, Twenty-Third and Forty-Eighth armies, as well as the local air-force units and a variety of ad hoc formations. A military council for Leningrad was formed at Stalin's insistance which included Zhdanov and Admiral N. G. Kuznetsov, amongst others. Meanwhile, Soviet forces, Fourth, Fifty-First and Fifty-Second armies, were gathering to cover the southern and western approaches to the Svir River and the town of Tikhvin to prevent the anticipated junction of the Germans and Finns.

Now AGN, reinforced by XXXIX Motorized Corps, prepared to make an all-out attack on Leningrad. This powerful corps' 18th and 20th Motorized divisions and 12th Panzer Division crashed through Forty-Eighth Army's defences on 25 August, backed up by the Stukas of Fliegerkorps VIII. As bombs and tanks shredded his men, Popov frantically pulled troops from quieter sectors but with his left flank in ribbons this was a risky move. Within four days 20th Motorized Division had reached the Neva River with 12th Panzer Division close by some days later. These two divisions were then ordered to widen the area around Shlisselburg and Lake Ladoga. The fall of Shlisselburg on 8 September completed the encirclement of Leningrad. It also marked the end of Voroshilov's involvement with the city: Stalin, disgusted with hearing the news of its fall from a German communiqué, resolved to sack his old friend. Zhukov was his replacement and, adhering strictly to Stalin's instructions, he demanded counter attack after counter attack in all areas. The Leningrad Military Council promised execution to anyone who retreated along with their families. Eighth Army tried but failed and was cut off in the bridgehead it would hold for over two years. But precious time was gained and the resources of AGN further worn down.

After a week of see-saw attack and counter attack, Mga station was captured as were the Siniavino Heights. To the west Krasnoe Selo, the former summer residence of the Tsars, was occupied by elements of XXXI Motorized Corps who then pressed on to reach the Pulkovo Heights on 12 September.

However, thanks to aggressive defensive fighting the highest areas around the observatory remained in Soviet hands. The Pulkovo crossroads, terminus of the Leningrad tram system's south-western line, was captured. In peacetime, for the price of a few kopecks, anyone could have travelled the 11km into the city centre.

The third week of September witnessed a series of remarkable defensive actions. At Uritsk naval infantry, with a handful of KV-1 tanks fresh off the production line of the Kolpino factory, held 58th Infantry Division. At Kolpino a local DNO force fighting alongside some regulars held off two German infantry divisions less than 8km from the famous Kirov factory, which was an essential plant manufacturing and repairing tanks throughout the siege of Leningrad. Now, however, von Leeb was deprived of much of his panzer and motorized resources, which were diverted to the south to participate in Operation Typhoon, which, it was anticipated, would culminate in the capture of Moscow. As Hitler had proclaimed on 22 September, 'I have no interest in the further existence of this large city after the defeat of Soviet Russia . . . We propose to blockade the city tightly and erase it from the earth by means of artillery fire and continuous bombardment from the air.' It was clear to von Leeb that his depleted force would be unable to mount major offensive operations and he requested of the Führer that AGN be permitted to go over to the defensive.

Although the city was now surrounded, it was not encirclement in depth. Both von Leeb and Stavka realized that measures must be taken to either firm up the siege lines or break them. And the Russian winter was coming.

(Above) Mussolini's (seen here to the left of Hitler) Italy contributed over 200,000 troops to Army Group South but only 4 MAS torpedo boats to the ill-fated Axis Naval Detachment K that operated on Lake Ladoga. (Nik Cornish at Stavka)

At midday on 22 June 1941 Molotov, the Commissar for Foreign Affairs and Stalin's right-hand man, broadcast to the USSR announcing the German invasion. It was noted at the time that his voice was 'faltering, slightly stuttery'. The message was one of German deceit and perfidy but ended, 'Victory will be ours'. (From the fonds of the RGAKFD at Krasnogorsk via Nik Cornish)

A PzKpfw 35(t) passes a farmhouse in Lithuania during the early days of Operation Barbarossa. This Czech-built vehicle was on the establishment of 6th Panzer Division and already obsolete in 1941. As part of XLI Panzer Corps, the division suffered heavy casualties in the fighting along the Luga River in August 1941. The division was transferred to Army Group Centre in late September for the drive on Moscow, thus depriving AGN of one of its few armoured units. (Nik Cornish at Stavka)

A KV-2 Soviet Heavy Assault Tank, designed as a 'bunker buster' not for tank-to-tank combat. Disabled by German fire, it was probably part of 2nd Armoured Division, XII Mechanized Corps which was engaged in the fighting in Lithuania as part of the North Western Front. Production of this type ended in October 1941. (Nik Cornish at Stavka)

However, the advancing German forces did not enjoy a run of alloyed success on the road to Leningrad. A BMW R12 motorcycle combination from the reconnaissance battalion of SS Division Totenkopf captured near Daugavpils, the second city of Latvia. During this period a complaint was lodged with the corps commander regarding the behaviour of Totenkopf men following the capture of Kraslava in early July. (Courtesy of the Central Museum of the Armed Forces Moscow via Nik Cornish)

Posed beneath images of Stalin and Lenin Soviet officers await interrogation. The haul of POWs taken by AGN was nowhere near as impressive as those of Army Group Centre and Army Group South. This was due as much to von Leeb's more cautious approach to far-ranging pincer movements as to the almost primeval nature of the terrain. (Nik Cornish at Stavka)

In late June Popov received authorization to raise People's Militia Divisions (DNO) from Leningrad's civilian population. Zhdanov appealed for fighters and some 160,000 volunteers came forward to fill the ranks of eight DNO. These formations took heavy casualties in the fighting in front of Leningrad. A total of 20 worker's battalions of 500 women apiece were created for the city's internal defence. One such unit is seen here crossing one of the city's many bridges. (Courtesy of TASS via Nik Cornish)

The flanks of the advancing panzer formations were to be guarded by the long-suffering infantry. Marching hundreds of kilometres over unmade roads took its toll on men and their horse-drawn transport. Of greater concern than blistered feet was the ever-present threat from Red Army units that were cut off but chose to fight on. The forests and marshes on the approaches were ideal ambush country, which the Soviets exploited at every opportunity. (Nik Cornish at Stavka)

As the supply lines of AGN grew ever longer and more tenuous forward units began to rely more and more on air supply. Here a unit of JU 52 transport aircraft lines up at an extemporized airfield to the west of Leningrad to airlift medical supplies, ammunition and fuel to the panzer spearheads. (Nik Cornish at Stavka)

These newly mobilized infantrymen, possibly a DNO formation, are heading for 1st Panzer Division's bridgehead at Sabsk on the Luga River. (From the fonds of the RGAKFD at Krasnogorsk via Nik Cornish)

Zhdanov mobilized over 200,000 civilians to work on the defensive system around Leningrad. As one remembered, 'women volunteers are camouflaging the trenches, artistically, masterfully, femininely'. (Courtesy of the Central Museum of the Armed Forces Moscow via Nik Cornish)

Pictured here in their *zeltbahn*, camouflage tent sections, two German scouts prepare for a mission to probe the Soviet defences south of Narva. For many of the German troops, more accustomed to an urban lifestyle, the eeriness and silence of the marshes and forests on the approaches to Leningrad conjured up images from Grimm's nastier fairy tales. Officers of the Totenkopf Division were allowed to remove their rank insignia to reduce casualties from well-concealed snipers. (Nik Cornish at Stavka)

A trophy of war pressed into service with the SS Totenkopf Division. This T-26 tank, marked with the white turret cross, was armed with a 45mm gun. Hundreds of Soviet armoured fighting vehicles were abandoned through lack of fuel or mechanical failure during the retreat to Leningrad. (Nik Cornish at Stavka)

A typical Red Army counter attack during the summer of 1941. The high command demanded that all German attacks be countered in the shortest possible time, regardless of the circumstances. Consequently, many were launched with little or no reconnaissance or artillery preparation. Needless to say, the price in blood was high. (Courtesy of the Central Museum of the Armed Forces Moscow via Nik Cornish)

One of the finest Soviet tanks the KV-1, ironically named in honour of Marshal Klim' Voroshilov, goes into action with close infantry support. At the outbreak of the war on the Eastern Front Soviet armoured doctrine was overwhelmingly in favour of close cooperation between infantry and tanks. This resulted in the commitment of small groups of tanks that were no match for the experience of the concentrations brought to bear by the Germans, despite the superiority of Soviet armour. (Courtesy of the Central Museum of the Armed Forces Moscow via Nik Cornish)

A column of German panzer IIIs negotiates a narrow causeway through a marshy forest to the west of Leningrad. The terrain through which AGN advanced became increasingly difficult for vehicles to cross the nearer it came to the city. The possibility of mines seeding tracks such as this was high. The crew are driving with the hatches open to reduce the temperature inside. (Nik Cornish at Stavka)

For the Finns the advance to their 1939 border was sufficient. They dug in during mid-September 1941, having achieved their prime objective. Their participation in the capture of Leningrad was not deemed crucial by the Germans. This Finnish machine-gun team is operating a Maxim gun model 1910 on its two-wheeled mounting. A simple and reliable weapon, it was ideally suited for the harsh terrain of Karelia. (Nik Cornish at Stavka)

Amidst the sand dunes part of the Baltic Fleet's coastal defences around their forward base at Libau in Latvia. The city was captured by 291st Infantry Division. Tragically, the dunes were also witness to the ghastly massacres perpetrated by Einsatzgruppen A that followed in the wake of AGN to carry out Hitler's racial policies. Alongside Latvian collaborators, the Germans killed upwards of 7,000 Jews in this area. (Nik Cornish at Stavka)

The view from the remains of the Pulkovo observatory. In November 1917 the Pulkovo Heights, which rise to over 300ft, had been the scene of Kerensky's only military adventure against the newly installed Bolshevik government. Kerensky's men got no further than Hitler's. The lenses and other equipment had been removed immediately prior to the German attack. (From the fonds of the RGAKFD at Krasnogorsk via Nik Cornish)

Stukas of Fliegerkorps VIII take off into the dawn in support of AGN's major push against Leningrad in September 1941. Due to its potency FK VIII was only deployed by order of Hitler or Goering. It was commanded by General Wolfram von Richthofen (he was a cousin of the Red Baron) who was a severe critic of von Leeb's prosecution of the campaign. When it was withdrawn Luftflotte I was AGN's only air asset. (Nik Cornish at Stavka)

Chapter Two

Blow and Backlash

The fall of Shlisselburg, the key city (as translated from German) in more than just name, marked the beginning of the siege (or Blockade as the Soviets and Russians term it) of Leningrad. But the events of 8 September did not mean that both sides settled down to a comfortable period of positional warfare despite the fact that AGN had begun its bombardment of Leningrad with heavy artillery on 4 September.

Von Leeb had encircled three armies, Twenty-Third, Forty-Second and Fifty-Fifth, inside the city, while Eighth Army licked its wounds in the Oranienbaum enclave. In total some 300,000 men in the remains of 20 divisions. But with his force reducing, from 15 September, in favour of Operation Typhoon von Leeb's options were limited. Fighting into the city, with all the perils that entailed, had been ruled out by Hitler himself on 6 September. Therefore, the choices von Leeb faced were the elimination of Oranienbaum, pushing east and north towards Volkhov and Tikhvin railway junctions or digging in for the winter. The latter was not a viable alternative, so he proposed his favourite plan to the Führer: a limited version of the Tikhvin–Volkhov offensive. The outcome of which von Leeb hoped would be the complete isolation of Leningrad other than by air and a link up with the dilatory Finns. Hitler instructed AGN to undertake a more ambitious version of the Tikhvin–Volkhov offensive utilizing XXXIX Motorized Corps to carry the main attack from Chudovo to Tikhvin. It was to begin on 16 October; two days after the first snow fell on Leningrad. However, AGN had been promised reinforcements: unfortunately, they were not armoured or motorized troops but two German infantry divisions from France, five battalions of paratroopers from Crete and 250th Infantry Division composed entirely of Spanish volunteers.

As AGN prepared so did Stavka. Not content to watch Lenin's city starve to death but not prepared to lose Moscow either, Stalin recalled Zhukov replacing him with Zhukov's favoured candidate, Major General I. I. Fediuninsky, an officer who enjoyed a bold, fighting reputation. This transfer was rapidly followed by another: Colonel General N. N. Voronov, the Chief of the Red Army Air Defence (PVO). Leningrad Front controlled one further army, Fifty-Fourth, which held the line from Lake Ladoga to Kirishi on the Volkhov River to the south-east. The Volkhov River ran from Lake Ilmen in almost a straight line to Lake Ladoga.

Its defenders from north to south, under the command of North Western Front, were Fourth Army, the Eastern Sector Operating Group (ESOG), Fifty-Second Army and the Novgorod Operating Group (NOG), the left flank of which rested on Lake Ilmen. This line was some 200km long with marsh on either bank for almost the whole of its length.

Fediuninsky's brief was straightforward: his men were to launch a pincer movement. ESOG would attack towards the west and link up with Fifty-Fourth Army. Flank support and supplementary attacks would be provided by the Neva Operational Group pushing out from the Leningrad pocket. It was anticipated that the result would be the liberation of the Shlisselburg corridor and the resumption of land supply lines to the city. The junction point for the pincers would be Siniavino. In total the Red Army would commit 70,000 men with 97 tanks and nearly 500 guns and Katyusha rocket launchers. Further support would be provided by aircraft of the Baltic Sea Fleet. The Soviets calculated that they faced some 55,000 Germans with a similar number of guns but few if any tanks. But once again the Red Army was pre-empted by von Leeb's attack, which began on 16 October regardless of snow up to 12in in depth. It was at that point the Soviets became aware of the German armour as 12th Panzer Division led off. Nonetheless, Stavka insisted that the offensive would commence on 20 October, as scheduled.

The previous four days of fighting had, however, weakened the line and a breach occurred in Fourth Army's front into which the panzers rolled, covering 60km in twelve days, quite an achievement across ground that thawed to the consistency of glue as often as it froze hard enough to support a tank. As the Germans expanded into the gap between Fourth and Fifty-Second armies, 12th Panzer and 20th Motorized divisions headed for Tikhvin as 21st and 26th Infantry divisions covered their left and right flanks respectively.

The German pressure on Fifty-Second Army forced it to withdraw to previously prepared positions where they remained. To fill the gap and protect Tikhvin Stavka committed four infantry and one tank division, but they were merely chewed up as they were fed piecemeal into the vacuum.

However, von Leeb's confidence was failing but Hitler, with eyes still fixed on Moscow, refused any further reinforcements, although troops were released by the postponement of an operation aimed at liquidating the Oranienbaum pocket.

Finally, after an almighty effort 8th and 12th Panzer divisions entered Tikhvin in the teeth of a blizzard on 8 November. The defenders scattered and were narrowly prevented from streaming panic stricken into the rear of Seventh Army facing the Finns. The German booty included an armoured train, which was fitting as the last rail link to the barge shipping points across Lake Ladoga was in their hands. The offensive towards Volkhov did not achieve its objective, slithering to a halt 15km before the town, as had the German attack at Kirishi. Only the Tikhvin salient could be judged a success but it was a fragile finger thrust into an increasingly substantial Soviet body. By now it was obvious that AGN had shot its bolt: its forces were massively overstretched and with the temperature falling to between -20 and -40 degrees Fahrenheit 'General Winter' was in command and Stavka was preparing to make the most of his favours.

Stavka placed General K. A. Meretskov in command of Fourth Army, called off Fifty-Fourth Army's attacks at Siniavino and realigned both armies' forces. With von Leeb's frontage east of the Volkhov River increased fivefold to roughly 350km, there was inevitably going to be a weak spot. Approximately 120,000 men with 100 armoured vehicles faced 190,000 Soviet troops with slightly fewer tanks. Stavka intended to launch a series of staggered attacks on the German line with the intention of building up to an all-out counter offensive over a period of a few weeks. Meretskov split his force into three groups. One would outflank Tikhvin to the north, one to the south, while the eastern group would link up with Fifty-Fourth Army. Fifty-Second Army and NOG would proceed to the Volkhov River and establish bridgeheads on the western bank. The latter's attack began on 12 November, Fourth Army's attack hit Tikhvin seven days later and Fifty-Fourth Army began on 4 December. The efforts of the NOG and Fifty-Second Army ground forward but slowly. However, operations against Tikhvin were encouraging; the German defences were beginning to buckle in the face of these unrelenting Soviet attacks and appalling weather. Von Leeb, fearful that 12th Panzer and 20th Motorized divisions would be cut off and destroyed, requested permission to abandon Tikhvin. Hitler grudgingly approved and the retreat to the Volkhov River began on 8 December, and was to be accomplished by 22 December. Eight days later Fifty-Second Army had driven the Germans back to the Volkhov River in the south. Meanwhile, Fifty-Fourth Army began to make progress supported by troops from Leningrad. AGN's I Army Corps was now in danger of being surrounded, however, Kirishi held and the situation eased.

On 1 December the Volkhov Front was formed, to be commanded by Meretskov, including the newly assembled Second Shock Army and Fifty-Ninth Army. Now Stavka, encouraged by the growing success of the offensive in front of Moscow, ordered the Volkhov and Leningrad fronts to 'raise the Leningrad Blockade'. Despite valiant efforts, by 30 December, the Red Army could push on no further than the bridgeheads over the Volkhov River. Breaking into Leningrad was tragically impossible and both fronts began to dig in. In his Christmas message to his troops, von Leeb summed up the achievements of AGN from June–December 1941: noting 438,950 POWs, 3,847 tanks and 4,590 guns taken or destroyed. But Leningrad had not fallen; its survival depended on the delicate balance of nature that determined the thickness of the ice now covering Lake Ladoga.

The first appearance of the Luftwaffe near the city was on 22 June 1941, when mines were dropped in the shipping lanes of Kronstadt. Until the arrival of Flieger-korps VIII, air support for AGN was Luftflotte I, led by Colonel General Alfred Keller. Such was the ferocity of the Soviet pilots, who often resorted to ramming enemy aircraft, Luftwaffe pilots commented it was easier flying over London. (Nik Cornish at Stavka)

Using the experiences of London, the Soviet air-defence system included 360 barrage balloons of the type seen here. The image shows the balloons being manhandled into position outside the front of the Drama Theatre on the Nevsky Prospect. Unfortunately, until 1942 radar was not in common use on the Leningrad Front. (From the fonds of the RGAKFD at Krasnogorsk via Nik Cornish)

The first super heavy artillery deployed by AGN consisted of three two-gun batteries of 24cm Skoda-built guns. Sited around the former Tsar's summer palace of Peterhof, the guns engaged ships of the Baltic Fleet as well as targets inside in the city. Manned by men of 84th Artillery Regiment, they took up positions during September. (Nik Cornish at Stavka)

The effect of artillery fire. (Courtesy of the Central Museum of the Armed Forces Moscow via Nik Cornish)

The provision of a stable base for the Skoda guns was essential. Here crew members move the left-hand earth box into position from its trailer. Two such boxes were required for each gun. A skilled team could, assuming the holes for the boxes were excavated, assemble boxes and gun in four hours thirty minutes. (Nik Cornish at Stavka)

As the German noose tightened around the city men found themselves defending their place of work. Here a detachment of an unidentified DNO assembles outside the Kirov factory. They are all uniformed and armed which was rarely the case during the early days of these units. (Courtesy of TASS via Nik Cornish)

Officers pause from following the action to pose for the camera as 61st Infantry Division occupies the Baltic Islands off the coast of Estonia. Clearing the archipelago took from 13 September–22 October. Although it distracted from the drive on Leningrad, it was deemed necessary for German civilian morale as bomber raids had been mounted on Berlin from Saaremaa Island. (Nik Cornish at Stavka)

Another Skoda product, the PzKpfw 38(t), negotiates a road muddied by thawing snow during the push towards Tikhvin by XXXIX Motorized Corps. The narrow tracks on Wehrmacht armour proved a severe disadvantage in such conditions as weight distribution was poor. The wider tracked Soviet armour did not have this problem. (Nik Cornish at Stavka)

Neatly photographed from the cover of a downed German bomber, a group of Soviet infantrymen break cover to advance around Tikhvin during November 1941. (From the fonds of the RGAKFD at Krasnogorsk via Nik Cornish)

An additional winter-specific weapon in the Soviet arsenal was the Aerosan. Powered by an obsolete aeroplane engine, these early snowmobiles were used to tow ski troops and for liaison and communications. Poor cross-country capabilities limited them to open ground or frozen rivers. In deep snow they could achieve speeds of up to 25mph. The model shown here is the NKL-26. (Courtesy of the Central Museum of the Armed Forces Moscow via Nik Cornish)

Spanish gunners operate a 10cm field gun in the rubble of Grigorovo near Novgorod. As part of the Sixteenth Army they were assigned a 56km sector of the front to hold along the Volkhov River, just north of Lake Ilmen. They arrived on 12 October having marched over 800km from Poland. Numbering over 15,000 officers and men, the division was a welcome addition to AGN. (Nik Cornish at Stavka)

The five battalions of paratroopers brought in from Crete were, at the insistence of Herman Goering, beautifully equipped to face the rigours of a Russian winter. They were placed in the line on the Neva River south of Shlisselburg on 30 September. For the next 2 months they repelled numerous attacks, incurring over 2,500 casualties. (Nik Cornish at Stavka)

Re-supply during the first winter of the siege was a major problem for AGN. Thousands of horses, unused to the climate, died and a great reliance was placed on hardy local breeds. Here a convoy of locally impressed panji wagons make light work of the terrain. Note the swastika flag to indicate the drover's loyalties. (Nik Cornish at Stavka)

Bad as the men of AGN believed their situation to be it was nothing compared with the ever worsening crisis in the Leningrad pocket. Here a group of refugees waits for a bowl of food from an army kitchen. (Nik Cornish at Stavka)

Men of 20th Motorized Division in Tikhvin on one of the better weather days that they occupied the town. They are wearing extemporized snow-camouflage smocks, probably made from locally acquired sheets. The haul of POWs when the town fell was roughly 20,000, along with 179 guns. (Nik Cornish at Stavka)

Mortars were an important weapon in the densely forested, marshy land around Leningrad. Even the smallest, such as the 50mm model 1938 seen here, were effective. The result of the high-explosive round was multiplied considerably when it exploded in woods by the generation of wooden shrapnel from the surrounding from the trees. (Courtesy of the Central Museum of the Armed Forces Moscow via Nik Cornish)

Digging in for the Sixteenth and Eighteenth armies first involved snow and ice walls and then more permanent structures. This 37mm anti-tank gun crew has made the best use of camouflage sheets. However, this weapon was of little assistance against the heavier Soviet tanks such as the KV-1. (Nik Cornish at Stavka)

The Soviets endured similar conditions. Here warmly clad Soviet anti-riflemen are seen preparing to use their PTRD 14.5mm single shot, manually reloaded anti-tank rifles in an anti-aircraft role. Although useless against more aircraft, such pieces were effective against slow-moving reconnaissance aircraft such as the Feisler Storch. (Courtesy of the Central Museum of the Armed Forces Moscow via Nik Cornish)

Outside the besieged city the farmers prepared for the winter. Here an elderly couple digs up their cache of supplies, some of which would be smuggled through the lines to Leningrad. The black market in such goods thrived despite the efforts of both the Soviet and German authorities. Philanthropy was not always the guiding motive in such affairs. (From the fonds of the RGAKFD at Krasnogorsk via Nik Cornish)

Other German booty included armoured trains such as this BP-35 gun wagon, which formed part of an unidentified Soviet armoured train. Such equipment was usually repaired and pressed into service against its former owners, generally in an anti-partisan/railway protection capacity. (Courtesy of the Central Museum of the Armed Forces Moscow via Nik Cornish)

Chapter Three

Such a Closeness to Death – Civilian Life in Leningrad

The single most horrifying aspect of the siege of Leningrad was the hellish suffering undergone by the civilian inhabitants. Although the two most recent sieges of modern times, Przemysl, 1914–15 and Port Arthur, 1905, both involved the Russian army as besiegers and besieged respectively, nothing could have prepared them for the events that Operation Barbarossa unleashed. This was to be war of racial extermination, a haphazardly planned genocide. However, this aspect of the German war aims was unknown to the peoples of the Soviet Union until the realities of the Nazi occupation became tangible.

As the news of the German invasion spread during the morning of 22 June the men of the city reported to their mobilization points accompanied by volunteers hurrying to join up. The People's Militia Divisions were hurried off to the front line, which had, by mid-July, reached the Luga River. At the same time thousands of civilians were recruited to begin work on the city's defence lines. The driving force behind this flurry of activity was A. A. Zhdanov, secretary of the Communist Party's Central Committee and Leningrad's party chief. Zhdanov had taken up the reins of power following the assassination of his predecessor, Sergei Kirov, on 1 December 1934 and was a diehard Stalinist described by one historian as a 'loyal robot', one of Stalin's inner circle and later in his career powerful enough to be considered as Stalin's likely successor. That Zhdanov was ruthless went without saying as he had made a significant contribution to the terror of the 1930s. This aspect of his nature was reinforced in the order of 14 July 1941, penned by himself and Voroshilov, which threatened execution for anyone deserting the front or sowing panic. With the Germans 200km south of Leningrad and some 1,000,000 involved in the construction of defensive works and related activities as well as tens of thousands of refugees flooding into the region it was hardly a time for delicacy.

With the collapse of the Luga Line during August, Chudovo, on the main Moscow–Leningrad railway line, fell and the rail link was cut. By the end of the month Mga had also been taken, thus isolating the city by rail. On 20 August Zhdanov called for the training of the entire population in 'shooting, grenade throwing and street fighting, we shall turn the city into the fascist's grave'. Preparations for a fight to the death in the streets of Leningrad went ahead apace.

Bridges, factories and public buildings were mined and plans were laid for a fighting withdrawal to the islands that made up the northern part of Leningrad.

However, before the breaking of the Luga Line, when the Germans appeared to have been held, many Leningraders, including many in authority, became over confident and felt that it was unlikely that the invaders would reach the city. This overly optimistic view of the situation, coupled with the authorities' fear of appearing to lack faith in the armed forces and thus Stalin's leadership, led to a somewhat casual approach to the evacuation of industrial assets and skilled workers. Men who had left their workplaces to enroll in the DNO formations were replaced by women, who now began to fill the ranks of local air-defence units. These groups, known by their Russian acronym of MPVO, were responsible for air-raid warnings, fire fighting and enforcing the blackout regulations. By early September some 268,000 people were active in the MPVO.

With Marshal Voroshilov literally in the front-line trenches and Zhdanov volley firing orders in all directions, the situation, from Moscow, appeared chaotic and, therefore, Stalin dispatched Molotov and Malenkov to report on conditions there. Whilst they were there, searching for scapegoats should the city fall, Stalin wrote to them, 'I fear Leningrad will be lost through imbecilic folly!' Despite this, Zhdanov kept his place having confessed that he had lost his nerve during a bombardment. Zhukov replaced Voroshilov and his arrival seems to have galvanized Zhdanov to a higher level of ruthlessness to save his fiefdom.

When Shlisselburg fell and Leningrad, but for Lake Ladoga, was isolated it held 2,544,000 civilians, including 400,000 children defined as those under 12. The suburban population and those in the outlying districts of the besieged area added a further 450,000, thus a total of nearly 3,000,000 excluding the soldiers and sailors were caught up in the Blockade. Most of the civilians were already organized into paramilitary/civil-defence groups but they now had to be housed, cared for medically and above all fed.

Rationing had been introduced on 18 July in large urban areas such as Moscow, Kiev and Leningrad. On the basis of that system's allowances it was concluded that the city held roughly thirty days of supplies of meat, cereals and flour to feed the defenders and the civilians.

Unfortunately, there was no one organization in overall control of food stocks. Indeed, sugar and confectionary had been shipped out of the city as the German ring was closing in and some restaurants continued to function for sometime feeding people 'off the ration' until brought under official control. Hitler had decided to starve Leningrad into submission rather than fight his way in and, therefore, every little scrap counted if the city was going to hold out.

Rations had already been reduced on 2 September and they were cut again on 12 September. Traditionally, food reserves and allowances in besieged areas has been measured in terms of bread, and this will be the yardstick employed here. The staple bread ration was reduced to 450g for workers (those in factories), to 300g for employees (office workers) and children and to 250g for dependents, those who fell into neither of the other categories. Soldiers and sailors received a higher daily allowance in the front line, those in the rear, slightly less than the fighters. However inadequate these rations may seem they were hazardously over optimistic given the paucity of the stocks. In part this was due to the belief that a breakthrough was imminent. On 26 September bread and flour reserves stood at 35,000 tons and the daily requirement was 1,100 tons: enough bread for just over thirty days barring any destruction by the bombardment or losses due to theft and looting. When it became clear that no early lifting of the siege was likely food had either to be flown in or shipped across Lake Ladoga, and both routes were subject to aerial interdiction. Nevertheless, 45,000 tons of food came in on barges during October and November, plus a further 1,200 tons of high-calorie food-stuffs that was airflifted in during late November. Fuel and ammunition, 25,000 tons in weight, also arrived in this period.

Despite this valiant effort, under the leadership of D. V. Pavlov, rations continued to fall. On 23 September beer production ceased as the useful ingre-dients were re-allocated to the bakeries. By late November edible cellulose was introduced into loaves, constituting up to 50 per cent of the weight. In one of his many handwritten letters to Stalin Zhdanov noted, 'The worst is that the hunger is spreading.' Added to the diminishing stocks of fuel for domestic heating and electricity, it appeared that Hitler's hope that Leningrad would be starved into submission seemed less than wishful thinking.

Two little harbours, one newly created at Osinovets on the Leningrad shore of Lake Ladoga and the other Novaya Ladoga at the mouth of the Volkhov River, were the bases from which the supply fleet operated. From Osinovets to the city was a 55km journey over a dilapidated suburban railway line. However, with the cutting of the rail link from Tikhvin to Novaya Ladoga on 7 November supplies had to be driven some 320km through uninhabited, virgin forest at a snail's pace of less than 35km a day such was the nature of the 'road'. As the lake began to freeze and the Germans retained their grip on Tikhvin hope began to fade and people in the city began to die. On 15 November Lake Ladoga became impass-able for shipping. Although the idea of a road across the ice had been on the back burner for sometime it depended on the thickness of the ice. The first, horse-drawn, convoys crossed the ice on 20 November: but these provided little more than the malnourished corpses of the horses themselves for the city's larder. Two days later the first lightly loaded trucks crossed but it was impossible to move more than 800 tons during the whole of the next week by this method. The first route across the ice was the shortest at 30km and this was followed by a second which opened on 28 November. By late December the ice had reached 1m in thickness with a further 300mm of snow which made it safe for the heaviest of lorries and even tanks. The design of the road was such that it could be used for two-way traffic, twenty-four hours a day in almost any weather. But with upwards of 2,000 people a day dying in Leningrad from 'alimentary dystrophy', as starvation was known, Zhdanov and his deputy, A. A. Kuznetsov, took charge of the supply situation. Despite their efforts and those of the transport services 53,000 people died in Leningrad during December 1941, they fell dead in the streets, drifted into eternity in their beds or passed on at their work benches. Although some essential workers had been evacuated by air or rail their numbers were low, a paltry 35,000 during November and December. On 6 December the official go-ahead to leave the city on foot across Lake Ladoga was given but it was a disorganized exodus with little or no provision made for those desperate souls fleeing. Consequently, numberless thousands died of exposure, exhaustion or dropped through holes in the ice.

Those remaining in the city faced an uncertain future where hunger and cold, burst sewers and frozen water pipes were rapidly becoming the norm, as were the dead lying unburied under pitiful mounds of snow. Cannibalism, a crime not recognized under Soviet law, was widespread: often the recipients closed their eyes to a source of black-market meat, but those caught were summarily executed. Nor were such ghoulish criminals reported for the shame and humiliation would only serve to reduce even further the morale of a population that was already plumbing a dangerous low.

The 'Road of Life' sustained Leningrad throughout the worst period of the siege and rations began to increase, first on 24 January and again on 10 February. The return journeys of the supply convoy lorries began to include passengers, non-essential civilians. By the end of January 12,000 had left by this method, rising to over 200,000 in March. When the ice finally thawed over 500,000 people had used this route. The last supply convoys crossed the lake on 24 April, carrying a load, 65 tons, of spring onions, more symbolic than useful but food nevertheless and the harbinger of a new, vital, season's growth for the city's remaining inhabitants.

A further 450,000 evacuees were shipped out between May and November 1942. Alongside people factory equipment was removed. The remaining industrial units changed over to the repair instead of manufacture of guns and vehicles. But with a workforce so malnourished and diseased productivity was extremely low. It was estimated that 25 per cent of the workforce was too ill to work in June 1942.

Nevertheless, Leningrad had proven 'it could take it', it being whatever the invaders could throw at the city. Although the siege continued after the opening of the Shlisselburg corridor in January 1943, that event coupled with the decisive victory at Stalingrad gave the population cause for great celebration.

With a reduced population and a functioning rail link the Leningraders' rations were raised beyond that elsewhere in the USSR.

A proud local patriotism had developed following the ghastly winter of 1941/2 which led to suggestions that although Moscow should remain the capital of the Soviet Union, Leningrad should be elevated to the position of capital of the Russian republic. There was also a feeling of contempt for the Muscovites' behaviour when the whole city panicked in mid-October 1941; shops were looted, part membership cards were burnt and bureaucrats, regardless of official policy, fled. Leningrad had not replicated such scenes on anything approaching a similar scale, therefore it felt itself to be deserving of some form of recognition. Zhdanov for his part, despite his closeness to Stalin, found himself falling out of favour with the 'Boss's' inner circle. Although an alcoholic asthmatic, he had led Leningrad through its darkest hours to victory. It was precisely for that reason he fell from grace as Stalin reasserted his and the Party's power in the post-war Soviet Union. There was no place for any individual heroic personality other than Stalin himself after 1945, even such colossi as Zhukov had to undergo a reduction in status.

Although the term 'Hero City' had been used in the Soviet press from 1942 onwards, Leningrad was awarded this honorific formally during 1945, the first of several such cities to be thus recognized. What the million or more civilian dead thought of the honour will, of course, never be recorded. Further recognition was given to Leningrad on 30 November 1966 when the entire region was granted the Order of Lenin in acknowledgement of the population's valour. Tikhvin, Luga and the Volkhov region were also rewarded with honours.

Some 150,000 refugees made their way to Leningrad during the summer and autumn of 1941. The majority were Russians but some Soviet collaborators from the Baltic republics were amongst them. The vast majority of them made their way on foot as all available rolling stock was commandeered by the armed forces. (Courtesy of the Central Museum of the Armed Forces Moscow via Nik Cornish)

A senior Red Army officer approached one group of women digging and complimented them on the efforts they were making. Their reply was less pleasant, 'Yes we are digging well but you fellows are fighting badly.' Roughly 550km of anti-tank ditches were dug on the approaches to Leningrad. The low water table is evident in this photograph. (Nik Cornish at Stavka)

The evacuation of plant and machinery was at times slowed by the lack of heavy lifting plant. Here tools are removed from the Stankilov facility. (From the fonds of the RGAKFD at Krasnogorsk via Nik Cornish)

This shop on the corner of Starinevski Prospect is in the process of conversion into a strongpoint during September 1941. A city of wide streets and tall, solidly constructed buildings, Leningrad would have proved a very difficult arena for street fighting. (From the fonds of the RGAKFD at Krasnogorsk via Nik Cornish)

Fear of air raids led the authorities, during June and July, to evacuate children to places such as Gatchina and Luga which were felt to be far enough away to avoid any danger. However, both were in the path of the invaders and the evacuees had to be moved again. Unfortunately, in the confusion some were overlooked and separated from their hosts and guardians. (Nik Cornish at Stavka)

Clearing casualties from the streets in daylight was initially a traumatic spectacle for the lucky onlookers. These bodies are being removed from Vosstanya Square near the Moscow station. The teams responsible for such work were under orders to wash the blood from the pavement as soon as possible after the event. (From the fonds of the RGAKFD at Krasnogorsk via Nik Cornish)

Members of the Komsomol (Young Communists) armed with sub-machine guns patrol the streets. Groups such as these were deployed to provide a rapid-reaction force to any landing by German paratroopers and to deter looters or other criminal elements. (From the fonds of the RGAKFD at Krasnogorsk via Nik Cornish)

Maintaining a clean, reliable supply of water was as essential to the city's survival as the food its inhabitants ate. Here a pump empties a shell crater so that the water mains can be repaired. By February 1942 1,500,000 typhoid inoculations had been administered. (From the fonds of the RGAKFD at Krasnogorsk via Nik Cornish)

25 October Prospect in autumn 1941. As supplies of fuel other than wood began to disappear so did trees, as log-gathering teams cut down as much timber as possible to provide fuel. In October the only establishments permitted electricity were the General Staff offices and the Smolny Institute, where the HQ of the Leningrad Defence Council and the city Soviet were located. (From the fonds of the RGAKFD at Krasnogorsk via Nik Cornish)

Hundreds of thousands of concrete 'dragon's teeth' anti-tank obstacles were laid along obvious roads and tracks that German armour would use. Their purpose was to slow an armoured attack, divert the tanks and allow the anti-tank gunners the opportunity for a clear shot. (From the fonds of the RGAKFD at Krasnogorsk via Nik Cornish)

Announcements were frequently made to the population by means of wall papers such as those seen here. The central list shows the latest ration instructions. (From the fonds of the RGAKFD at Krasnogorsk via Nik Cornish)

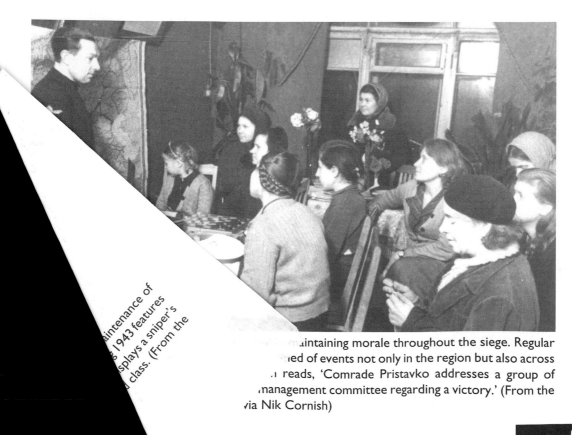

...aintenance of ...g 1943 features ...splays a sniper's ... class. (From the

...aintaining morale throughout the siege. Regular ...ed of events not only in the region but also across ... reads, 'Comrade Pristavko addresses a group of ...management committee regarding a victory.' (From the ...ia Nik Cornish)

Youngsters enjoy the snow. Between January and May 1942 30,000 orphans were placed in 85 new children's homes. The majority of their parents had died in the famine of that first horrific winter. (From the fonds of the RGAKFD at Krasnogorsk via Nik Cornish)

A Soviet guardsman enjoys a smoke. Tobacco was also rationed, leading to all manner of substitutes being devised. These included the smoking of hops and maple leaves. Rarely if ever would a smoker exchange his or her ration of tobacco for food. (Courtesy of the Central Museum of the Armed Forces Moscow via Nik Cornish)

Fostering the relationship between defenders and their charges was vital to the m
morale. Visits to the quieter areas of the front line were encouraged. This one durin
ladies from the Oktobersky district speaking to Captain Grigoriev, who proudly d
rifle. Grigoriev was a recent recipient of the Order of the Patriotic War secon
fonds of the RGAKFD at Krasnogorsk via Nik Cornish)

Two generations of the Amelkin family sit amidst the ruins of their apartment. Although reduced in ferocity, the German bombardment continued. This photograph is dated 20 August 1943. (From the fonds of the RGAKFD at Krasnogorsk via Nik Cornish)

Tickets for a performance of Dmitri Shostakovich's *Seventh Symphony* being sold in 1942. The symphony, nicknamed the 'Leningrad', was adopted as a symbol of the city's resistance. The first performance in the city took place on 9 August 1942 and was broadcast throughout the city on the public-address system. Govorov, commander of the Leningrad Front, ordered an artillery barrage to silence the Germans during the performance. (From the fonds of the RGAKFD at Krasnogorsk via Nik Cornish)

Decorating the streets to celebrate the official raising of the siege on 27 January 1944. (From the fonds of the RGAKFD at Krasnogorsk via Nik Cornish)

An interrupted funeral. As the ground thawed it became possible to bury more bodies. Not all remained at peace. (From the fonds of the RGAKFD at Krasnogorsk via Nik Cornish)

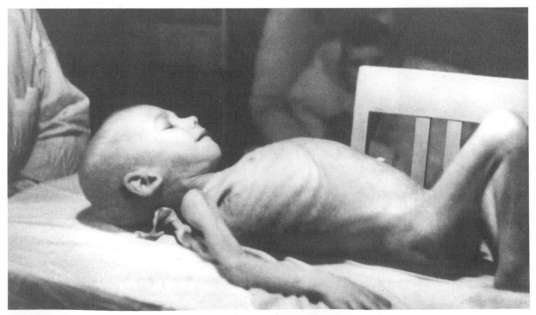

A victim of German 'Kultur' and alimentary dystrophy. (Courtesy of TASS via Nik Cornish)

Chapter Four

The Grand Design

The achievements of the Red Army's counter offensive and the liberation of Tikhvin and Rostov emboldened both Stavka and Stalin, who were determined to build on these successes to 'pave the way for the complete destruction of Hitlerite forces in 1942'.

The Leningrad, Volkhov and North Western fronts were therefore to carry out the defeat of AGN and raise the siege of Leningrad. The primary role in the latter phase of this operation would rest on the shoulders of Meretskov's Volkhov front, which would receive substantial reinforcements. Again, it would be an offensive based on pincer movements. The almost fresh Second Shock and Fifty-Ninth armies were to head west to cut the Leningrad–Dno–Novgorod railway line having crossed the Volkhov River. Fifty-Fourth Army (Leningrad Front), outside the city, would meet up with these two and, having driven the Germans out of Lyuban and Chudovo, proceed north-westwards to link up with other units of the Leningrad Front to break the Blockade. At the front the attacking armies' flanks would be covered by Fourth Army and mount diversionary attacks to pin German reserves.

Leningrad Front's (now commanded by Major General M. S. Khozin) Fifty-Fifth Army was to break out of the city, capture Tosno to the south of Shlisselburg, thus cutting the German line of retreat. Supplementary attacks would be launched from Oranienbaum and from elsewhere in the Leningrad defence lines.

North Western Front's Eleventh Army was to liberate Staraia Russia and join hands with Fifty-Second Army thereby clearing the Novgorod *oblast*. The Third and Fourth Shock armies, in conjunction with the Kalinin and Western fronts to the south, would recapture the Rhzev and Viazama *oblasts*. The final act in this grand design for the theatre north of Moscow would be undertaken by Thirty-Fourth Army, which was to eliminate German forces in and around Demiansk. To carry out this gigantic operation over 400,000 Soviet troops would be committed with a further 250,000 in reserve.

Inevitably, the weather delayed the assembly of units and the first attack by Fourth, Fifty-Second and Fifty-Ninth armies finally began on 6 January. A day later Second Shock Army joined the fray.

Unfortunately for Meretskov his forces were still incomplete. Although the Soviet troops went forward, the coordination of attacks began to erode almost from the outset. As Fifty-Eighth Army struggled to expand its bridgehead reserves were committed in dribs and drabs. When Second Shock Army was sent in as support it lost 3,000 men in 3 minutes – not even as ruthless a dictator as Stalin had the manpower to sustain such a butcher's bill and the attack was halted after 2 days. Fifty-Fourth Army faired equally badly at Kirishi, a pattern tragically followed by the other armies of Leningrad Front, who made no more than a couple of kilometres progress for which they paid a heavy toll in blood and equipment. The picture on North Western Front was brighter; Demiansk was encircled and the suburbs of Staraia Russia reached. Enraged, Stalin ordered a resumption of operations across the entire area and to ensure his field commanders spared no effort, sent as his personal representative with the power of life and death from highest to lowest Colonel General L. Z. Mekhlis, the senior Red Army Political Officer who had already purged Thirty-Fourth Army's senior commanders during the retreat across the Baltic States in the summer and autumn of 1941. The offensive, finally with the bulk of its heavier artillery in place, recommenced on 13 January. For three days Second Shock Army battered its way a small distance into the German defence system. Its flank guards, Fourth and Fifty-Second armies, made no headway at all and once again assumed defensive postures after two days. In an effort to rekindle its offensive spirit Fifty-Fourth Army was split in two and a new Eighth Army created, led by Major General A. V. Sukhomlin. But still there was no improvement.

By 17 January Second Shock Army had pushed almost 10km into the German lines but strong positions on either side of the penetration channelled the advance. Whilst Second Shock Army struggled valiantly to expand the neck of this incursion Meretskov gambled on its success and sent XIII Cavalry Corps supported by an infantry division into the breach in an attempt to break through into the rear of AGN's Sixteenth Army. As the Germans responded to this threat they still maintained a powerful grip on the neck of the funnel despite the almost suicidal attacks launched by elements of Fifty-Second and Fifty-Ninth armies. Nevertheless, the integrity of the German line south-east of Leningrad was in jeopardy.

Next, Meretskov ordered Second Shock Army to swing east to take Lyuban and join up with Fifty-Fourth Army. This move was to be spearheaded by the cavalry, who would ignore points of resistance leaving them to be dealt with by the following infantry – it was Blitzkrieg without the tanks. With almost 100,000 men in the funnel behind their lines it was essential that the Germans maintain their grip on its neck and this they succeeded in doing, even as the Soviet cavalry were now operating over 70km to their rear. Maybe during the summer Stalin's horsemen could have made the journey to Lyuban in two days but the winter was abnormally severe and their ride reduced to a crawl. The slow pace of the advance enabled Field Marshal G. W. von Kuchler, von Leeb's successor earlier in January, to exploit his internal lines of communications to transfer forces from quieter sectors of AGN's line. From Sixteenth Army XXXVIII Army Corps secured the southern flank of Second Shock Army's funnel, whilst Eighteenth Army committed five army infantry divisions and the 4th SS Polizei Division to secure the northern flank. As these units moved into place on 12 February the strongpoints either side of the funnel's neck fell into Soviet hands, expanding the breach to over 14km through which Meretskov poured yet more men. Now within striking distance of Lyuban the fighting ebbed and flowed as both sides fed in reserves.

Stalin, still dissatisfied with the slow pace of the advance, ordered a re-drafting of the plans. The alterations were modest: Fifty-Fourth Army was reinforced to give it fresh striking power to reach Lyuban. Now with powerful air support Fifty-Fourth Army made ground reaching to within 10km of its objective. A total of eight German divisions now faced encirclement. With a further 90,000 trapped in Demiansk and over 5,000 penned in Kholm, not only AGN but Smolensk and the rear of Army Group Centre were in grave danger. But now the only strong formations available to Stavka were those of North Western Front engaged around Demiansk. However, the Germans trapped there had to be eliminated before North Western Front could deploy its forces to the north and this did not happen. The Demiansk pocket was successfully supplied by air and held out until relieved in late April 1942.

Nor was Demiansk the only light on AGN's horizon. Von Kuchler, with Hitler's blessing, planned what was known as Operation Beast of Prey (Raubeiter). Its objective was to slice through the neck of the Lyuban funnel, isolate and then destroy Second Shock Army. The counter offensive began on 15 March. 58th Infantry and 4th SS Polizei divisions attacked the neck of the funnel and by 20 March had linked up. Notwithstanding its isolation, Second Shock Army doggedly pursued its goal of reaching Lyuban. Simultaneously, Meretskov launched bloody counter attacks to re-open the supply lines, which he succeeded in doing on 27 March. But then the weather changed, the thaw came as did the rain and the efficiency of the supply link was reduced to almost nil allowing only men on foot to traverse its artillery swept opening. With few if any supplies getting through the situation for Second Shock Army became grave. Almost overnight the operations of Volkhov and Leningrad fronts stopped. Trapped in a fast-thawing swamp, Second Shock Army and the other units would have to wait for relief. They provided a fine target for German aircraft and artillery.

Stavka reacted swiftly but strangely. Lieutenant General M. S. Khozin took over both Leningrad and Volkhov fronts and was charged with mounting a rescue mission to save Second Shock Army. In an effort to bolster the morale of the isolated troops Lieutenant General A. A. Vlasov was flown into the pocket on 20 April, Hitler's 53rd birthday, to take charge. His arrival did not materially affect the situation. Khozin launched several localized attacks enabling groups of Soviet troops to escape.

However, the major operations were now at an end. The losses sustained by the Red Army were not compensated for by the gains and still there was no land route into Leningrad. As Lake Ladoga thawed and the 'Road of Life' disappeared into the murky depths the city was again solely dependent on the barges and ferries for the bulk of its foodstuffs.

As the first shoots of spring began to appear above the firming ground both Stalin and Hitler reviewed their options. The fate of Leningrad hung in the balance.

The term 'Shock' was applied to the armies or lesser units that were to head an assault. They were strengthened with 'bolt-on' specialist formations such as combat engineers and automatic weapons battalions, such as the men seen here. Almost all are armed with SVT-40 automatic rifles. (Courtesy of the Central Museum of the Armed Forces Moscow via Nik Cornish)

An mg 34 team prepares to open fire. An excellent weapon, it had an unfortunate habit of jamming when used in snow or muddy conditions. It was doubtless responsible for a high percentage of Soviet infantry casualties as the Red Army still tended to attack in long, highly visible waves. (Nik Cornish at Stavka)

Stug III assault guns such as these formed a vital element in AGN's anti-tank defences. Originally conceived as an infantry support weapon, the Stug III came into its own as an anti-tank weapon. Assault Gun Battery 667 received a supply of anti-tank shells and in two days accounted for nine Soviet KV and T-34 tanks. (Nik Cornish at Stavka)

Despite horrific casualties the Soviet infantry kept coming. Casualty evacuation was not a refined art during the first winter campaign in the USSR. Here well-equipped men of Second Shock Army move up to their jump-off positions. With negligible air support progress was slow. (Courtesy of the Central Museum of the Armed Forces Moscow via Nik Cornish)

For the recently arrived Spaniards of 250th Infantry Division the fighting at Novgorod was an horrific baptism of fire. By early 1942 the division had suffered over 2,000 casualties. This young recruit has just received his Christmas gift parcel courtesy of Franco's government. The Spanish dictator ensured his men were well provided for throughout their time on the Leningrad Front. (Nik Cornish at Stavka)

Soviet tank men (left) share a meal with some infantrymen of 305th Rifle Division that penetrated the German lines on 7 January. Poor coordination between the various arms of service frequently negated the bravery of the men themselves, who often had relatives trapped in Leningrad. The infantryman at the rear is wearing the old-style Red Army hat, the Budenovka, which featured a large red star on the front that served as fine target for German marksmen. (Courtesy of the Central Museum of the Armed Forces Moscow via Nik Cornish)

Despite the failure of supporting formations to expand the pocket growing around Second Shock Army, Volkhov Front's XIII Cavalry Corps poured into the area in order to renew the impetus of the advance. German strongpoints such as Spaskaya Polist and Zemiitsy at the neck of the pocket held firm. (Courtesy of the Central Museum of the Armed Forces Moscow via Nik Cornish)

One of the most useful and successful extemporized Soviet ZIS-30, which consisted of an artillery tractor armed with a ZIS 57mm M41 anti-tank gun. The ZIS 57mm gun was capable of penetrating the armour of any German tank at this time. As can be seen, there was little in the way of protection for the crew plus it used fuel at a dramatic rate. However, it was an excellent performer in rough and swampy terrain. Several batteries of this tank destroyer were transferred to the Volkhov Front. (Courtesy of the Central Museum of the Armed Forces Moscow via Nik Cornish)

A German outpost of 291st Infantry Division keeps watch over the southern approaches to Lyuban. AGN's assets were spread dangerously thin forcing von Leeb to commit his only rear security division, 285th, to the front line. The security divisions were weak in numbers and lacked any anti-tank guns. However, their often over age and unfit men were capable of defending fixed points in a supporting role. (Nik Cornish at Stavka)

The less than subtle Katyusha multiple rocket launcher was available to Volkhov Front, but arrived late because of the grim condition of the roads as it was truck mounted it. The weapon was top secret, operated by the NKVD (the secret police with responsibility for internal and border security forces) in what were designated Guards Mortar formations. Despite its inaccuracy, the Katyusha (officially the BM-13) fired up to sixteen rockets of 130mm calibre and proved valuable in providing much-needed fire support as artillery heavier than 76mm was rare on this front. (Courtesy of the Central Museum of the Armed Forces Moscow via Nik Cornish)

Men of the 4th Separate Ski Battalion, which numbered roughly 1,600 of all ranks, move out in February 1942. One of Fifty-Fourth Army's 'bolt-on' units, these specialist troops had no German equivalent in the Leningrad theatre. Silent and deadly, they were much feared by the men of AGN, particularly those on lonely outpost duty during the hours of darkness. (Courtesy of the Central Museum of the Armed Forces Moscow via Nik Cornish)

Unsurprisingly, the Germans deployed artillery in the direct-fire role along the flanks of the neck of Second Shock Army's supply line. The supply lines were nicknamed 'Erika' and 'Dora' by the Germans. Erika was to the north and Dora to the south. With a range of 12km, this 105mm field howitzer was capable of reaching both Erika and Dora. (Nik Cornish at Stavka)

Providing bread and other supplies for the troops advancing to Lyuban was a vast undertaking in itself. It was well-nigh impossible for the advancing Soviet troops to live off the land as it was frozen solid and the Germans had already foraged it clean. Only the cavalry mounts, hardy steppe-bred beasts like the one seen here, were capable of living comfortably in such harsh conditions. Transported in such a manner as this one can easily imagine the rock-hard condition of the bread. (Courtesy of the Central Museum of the Armed Forces Moscow via Nik Cornish)

A German position south of Lyuban. It was the extemporized defence system established in such locations as this that enabled AGN to hold much of its line along the Volkhov River. (Nik Cornish at Stavka)

Adapting rapidly to the wintry conditions was essential to the survival of AGN. One example of such a measure is the mounting of this 20mm anti-aircraft gun on a sledge. The gunner, warmly wrapped in his locally acquired shuba overcoat, is well supplied with ammunition. Equally useful against light armour and lethal against infantry, this weapon was mainly employed against ground targets during the winter of 1941/2 when conditions reduced air attacks to virtually nil. (Nik Cornish at Stavka)

Any operation by the Red Army during this period incurred high casualties. To make good these losses local men were often drafted into the ranks of the nearest formation. In many cases those liberated were Soviet troops who had hidden behind German lines during the period of retreat months earlier. They were a very useful addition to the infantry divisions that were bleeding white. Any investigation of their activities while absent would wait until the front became quieter and then it would be thorough. (Courtesy of the Central Museum of the Armed Forces Moscow via Nik Cornish)

As the progress of Second Shock Army slowed the advance on Demiansk grew more successful. One of the units encircled was the 3rd SS Division Totenkopf. However, not all its men reached the safety of their own lines. This SS man has been captured by a Soviet civilian, a member of the increasing number of partisan formations springing up behind AGN's lines. His fate, following interrogation, was predictable as both sides conducted the war mercilessly. (Courtesy of the Central Museum of the Armed Forces Moscow via Nik Cornish)

Civilians emerged from the forests and marshes to help their liberators. Here a group of women, pathetically clothed for the winter, gather up telephone wire. (Courtesy of the Central Museum of the Armed Forces Moscow via Nik Cornish)

A Soviet sniper in position high in the tree line takes a bead on his target. Priority shots were officers followed by NCOs and any specialists, such as signal-line repair crews. Such was their reputation and ability to themselves that the Germans often used light artillery to take them out. (Courtesy of the Central Museum of the Armed Forces Moscow via Nik Cornish)

Assembling the forces for Operation Beast of Prey, AGN's counter offensive, an assault battery receives ammunition before moving up to its start line in early March. But with the prospect of the thaw and the consequent *rasputitsa* (the time of mud) it was vital that von Kuchler moved fast to avoid becoming bogged down. (Nik Cornish at Stavka)

Chapter Five

Fire Magic and Northern Lights

Even Hitler, who had taken the role of Commander of the German army in December 1941, was aware that his forces on the Eastern Front were incapable of undertaking a massive operation across the whole length of the line. Therefore, despite a huge influx of reinforcements from Romania, Hungary and Italy, there was to be one major offensive, Operation Blue (Blau), the drive to the Caucasus. All other sectors in the USSR were to be sidelined. There were two major thorns in the Axis' side that needed to be tidied up – the ongoing sieges of Sevastopol and Leningrad. Consequently, OKH (the German High Command) decreed, with the Führer's approval, that they would postpone, 'the final encirclement of Leningrad . . . until . . . sufficient force permits'.

The planning of Operation Northern Lights (Nordlicht) had begun earlier in the year. It was an ambitious offensive that envisaged AGN's two armies, Sixteenth and Eighteenth, each mounting an offensive. Sixteenth Army would attack southwards, coordinating with AGC to eliminate the Soviet forces in and around Kholm thus relieving the pressure on Smolensk and AGC's rear. Eighteenth Army would breakthrough out of Pushkin into southern Leningrad, culminating in the occupation of the city. Planning on two minor operations, Beggar's Staff (Bettelstab) to deal with the Pogoste salient, and Moor Fire (Moorbrand) to liquidate the Oranienbaum bridgehead, now held by the Coastal Operations Group, was now also complete. Hitler agreed to send General Erich von Manstein's Eleventh Army and its siege train of super heavy artillery to facilitate Operation Northern Lights when its present mission, the capture of Sevastopol, was concluded.

Stavka's orders to Leningrad Front were for more immediate execution – Second Shock Army was to be rescued. Khozin (now commander of Leningrad Front) suggested that it would be sensible to combine the rescue mission with an operation to open up a land corridor by driving the Germans from the Siniavino region. Moscow agreed and began to dispatch reinforcements. Second Shock Army was expected to fight its way towards the relief force, which it would undertake from 20 May. To prevent Vlasov's escape Eighteenth Army was instructed to destroy it completely. By 31 May Second Shock Army was thoroughly cordoned off but continued to attack furiously.

Re-establishing the Volkhov Front on 8 June, Stalin replaced Khozin on the Leningrad Front with Lieutenant General L. A. Govorov. Despite these moves

Vlasov's troops still remained cut off and order rapidly collapsed during the course of the next four weeks.

At a meeting with Hitler von Kuchler ran his plans past the Führer, who decided to consider them. While the Commander in Chief of the German army debated, AGN held off several attacks in the Pogoste area, but the Soviet's efforts were not diminishing and it was becoming clearer that they were preparing for another major offensive. On 23 July Hitler announced his alterations to AGN's summer plans by insisting that Leningrad be taken by September that year. In brief, Northern Lights became Operation Fire Magic (Feurzauber). Operations Moor Fire and Beggar's Staff were to be undertaken promptly. However, Kuchler managed to convince Hitler that these operations were beyond the capabilities of AGN as it stood and it would therefore be necessary to await the arrival of Eleventh Army. In a calculatedly insulting move von Manstein was given operational control of Operation Northern Lights, as it had become once more and directly answerable to OKH over Kuchler's head with the remit to flatten Leningrad and meet up with the Finns. Von Manstein's HQ staff finally arrived in AGN on 27 August. However, by then the situation had altered radically.

During July Soviet intelligence noted German forces assembling between Chudovo and Siniavino which triggered Leningrad Front to carry out spoiling attacks. These were undertaken by Forty-Second and Fifty-Fifth armies and continued with the useful effect of drawing Eighteenth Army's assets to the threatened points. Stavka, however, wanted more – a complete pre-emptive offensive by both Volkhov and Leningrad fronts in the region Shlisselburg–Siniavino. Leningrad Front's Fifty-Fifth Army and Neva Operational Group would take Siniavino, connecting with Volkhov Front's Eighth Amy further west, while the reformed Second Shock Army would fight its way into Krasny Bor to meet forces moving out from Leningrad. The earlier attacks had forced Kuchler to use early arrivals from Eleventh Army to bolster his defences. The distance separating the attackers from Leningrad and Volkhov fronts was roughly 20km but marshes and forests benefitted the defenders, as events would show.

As if timed to perfection Manstein's arrival coincided with the opening of Volkhov Front's offensive – Eighth Army broke into the German lines at the boundary of 227th and 223rd Infantry divisions. The snail's pace of the advance brought them to the slopes of the Siniavino Heights some 6km from the rear of the German front on the banks of the Neva River facing Leningrad. But the penetration was narrow and the flanking units were unable to push through German strongpoints at its base. Additional forces were being fed into the area thus the defence was growing stronger. Incredibly, Meretskov repeated his mistakes of earlier in the year by committing his reserves in piecemeal fashion. On the banks of the Neva River Govorov's troops had established a shaky bridgehead, but could only just hold on let alone expand towards the Volkhov Front's spearhead, which was less than 5km away, when the Germans counter attacked at the base of Eighth

Army's salient. On 12 September 12th Panzer, 24th and 170th Infantry divisions attempted to cut off Eighth Army but failed. As the fighting continued von Manstein concentrated his forces and added two more infantry divisions and by 25 September had sliced through the neck of the salient. The following day Govorov, at heavy cost to the assault troops, managed to expand the Neva bridgehead but it was too late. The attack was contained by the forty tanks of 12th Panzer Division and Fifty-Fifth Army pulled back across the river within a few days.

On 29 September Stavka ordered Volkhov Front to pull out of the Siniavino pocket. Thousands of Soviet troops managed to escape through the German lines. However, in keeping with his aggressive reputation, Meretskov pleaded with Stavka to allow him to try again. Finally, on 3 October he was refused permission to do anything more than take up defensive positions and allow his men some much needed respite.

During this period of activity von Manstein had modified the overall strategy for Operation Northern Lights. The emphasis was shifted from penetrating Leningrad itself to one of encirclement. Having noted the tenacity of Soviet troops during the final stages of the Sevastopol opewaration, he decided to opt for a wider ranging envelopment of the city by crossing the Neva River some 16km south-east of Leningrad and sweeping up into the rear of Twenty-Third Army that faced the Finns.

Thus isolated from all but air supply Leningrad would therefore be simply starved into submission. To carry out this plan von Manstein requested some 10,000 replacements as the divisions of Eleventh Army had been significantly eroded by the recent fighting. Furthermore, mopping-up operations were going slowly resulting in further casualties. Indeed, Soviet troops would remain at large in the pocket until late October.

As the Soviets dug in so too did von Manstein's forces. From 14 October AGN resumed the defensive. Operation Northern Lights was postponed and Hitler instructed von Manstein to use his now fully assembled siege train to batter Leningrad into surrender. The bulk of Eleventh Army was to be transferred to AGC commencing in late October, as were divisions from Eighteenth Army. Once again the siege had become a sideshow, a point heavily underscored when von Manstein and his HQ staff were rushed south to deal with the crisis developing along the Volga River at Stalingrad.

While the fighting on land had reduced in ferocity the Red Banner Baltic Fleet had become more active. Soviet submarines had sortied into the Baltic Sea, sinking over 50,000 tons of shipping. In order to prevent such an episode recurring and threatening Swedish iron-ore shipments to the Reich a 48km anti-submarine net was laid across the outlet from the Gulf of Finland. This, along with an increase in the minefields, effectively penned the submarines until the autumn of 1944. This did not prevent the capital ships from providing invaluable supporting fire to land operations from the relative safety of the Neva River and Kronstadt. Heavy naval guns from the training and proving grounds were also pressed into service.

Men of North Western Front's First Shock Army patrol the edges of the Ramushevo corridor between the main German lines and the Demiansk pocket. It was through this gap in the lines that supplies were moved as well as the air bridge. A breakout attempt widened this corridor in late March. Very little of the terrain in this region was as open as seen here. (From the fonds of the RGAKFD at Krasnogorsk via Nik Cornish)

Towards the end of the encirclement of Demiansk a JU 52 transport plane takes on a load of wounded including an SS stretcher case. It was the success of this airlift that encouraged Hitler and Goering cheerfully to promise the same level of support to Sixth Army in Stalingrad nine months later. However, over 100 JU 52 aircraft were lost. The Kholm and Demiansk pockets only required 265 tons of supplies, whereas Sixth Army required 800. Furthermore, North Western Front's air strength and anti-aircraft capabilities were low. (Nik Cornish at Stavka)

General A. A. Vlasov, former hero of the Moscow defence (and like Stalin a former trainee for the priesthood), became the convenient scapegoat for the loss of Second Shock Army. Vlasov was captured by AGN on 12 July 1942, apparently betrayed by a local farmer. Vlasov went on to form the Russian Liberation Army (ROA) that fought for the Germans. Captured by the Soviets in 1945, he was executed in 1946. (Nik Cornish at Stavka)

A major problem for the Germans throughout the area under AGN's control was clean water. The native solutions were often simple, as seen here, but effective. For the sensitive central European digestive system more thoroughgoing processes were essential to prevent epidemics of dysentery or typhoid. (Nik Cornish at Stavka)

General Erich von Manstein, seen here in the siege lines around Sevastopol, was familiar with the Leningrad Front having served with AGN at the start of the siege. The greater part of Germany's super heavy artillery had been committed to the reduction of Sevastopol. Now much of it would be brought to bear on Leningrad. Eleventh Army began to move north when Sevastopol fell on 4 July. (Nik Cornish at Stavka)

Men of the 4th SS Division Polizei go out on patrol. As well as their camouflage smocks, they are well provided with anti-mosquito nets to deter insect attack in the swamps around the city and along the banks of the Neva River. This division was recruited from police reservists and formed in 1939. Its equipment was often foreign, such as the robust, efficient Czech-made ZB-53 machine guns seen here. Never regarded as an elite formation, it was transferred from AGN in the spring of 1943. (Nik Cornish at Stavka)

Amongst the siege guns Manstein would bring were French railway guns similar to the one seen here, a 240mm piece. The siege batteries were under the command of HArKo (Higher Artillery Command) 303. They were to have been deployed to neutralize the artillery on Kronstadt Island naval base which supported the Oranienbaum bridgehead. However, limited ammunition restricted their value. (Nik Cornish at Stavka)

The Oranienbaum enclave had assumed the mantle of bridgehead by the spring of 1942. The designation of Eighth Army had been transferred to a unit on the Volkhov Front. Now known as the Coastal Operational Group, it was well dug in and demanded the attention of German forces to the rear of the main front every time there was an offensive by either side. It was foolish of the Germans to ignore it for so long. Here an anti-tank rifle covers what is doubtless a heavily mined section of road. (From the fonds of the RGAKFD at Krasnogorsk via Nik Cornish)

With the coming of spring nature revealed the losses suffered by the Volkhov and North Western fronts. These T-26 light tanks were abandoned by their crews due to lack of fuel. The machine guns have probably been removed, obviously to arm the crew. It is possible these tanks were part of 122nd Tank Brigade, part of Fifty-Fourth Army. (Nik Cornish at Stavka)

The terrain which 8th and 12th Panzer divisions were to operate was, as Hitler said, unsuitable in many areas. The engineer units of AGN had to build hundreds of kilometres of corduroy road such as this. Based on silver birches, the exhausted engineers, swathed in mosquito nets, watch as PzKpfw IV drives gingerly forward. At least the short 75mm gun was unlikely to get snagged in the undergrowth. (Nik Cornish at Stavka)

One of the first arrivals from Eleventh Army was 5th Mountain Division. The mountain troops were placed in support of the forces along the Siniavino Heights. Here a 105mm mountain gun is prepared to fire. During the summer period this division suffered some 2,000 casualties and lost over 25 per cent of its horses, reducing its mobility severely. (Nik Cornish at Stavka)

Meretskov, not wishing to repeat the mistakes of the winter offensive, developed a considerable weight of heavy artillery. A gun and tractor, so heavily camouflaged as to be unrecognizable, moves up to the front, much to the delight of local children while one gunner cheerfully salutes the cameraman. During the 1942 summer offensive Soviet artillery spotting had become more sophisticated than earlier in the year. However, it was still well below what was necessary. (Courtesy of the Central Museum of the Armed Forces Moscow via Nik Cornish)

An abandoned BT-7 is casually inspected by men of 170th Infantry Division, newly arrived from the Crimea. Eighth Army's 124th lost twenty-four out of twenty-seven tanks when they became bogged down in a swamp. They were destroyed piecemeal by the Germans. (Nik Cornish at Stavka)

The armoured forces of AGN received the first Tiger I unit committed to the front when Heavy Tank Battalion 502 arrived in late August. Their first action was on 29 August, although two broke down almost immediately. Nevertheless, their appearance contributed significantly to slowing down the Soviet attack on Siniavino. The 88mm gun was more than capable of knocking out any enemy tank in the theatre. Even immobile they were deadly defence positions. (Nik Cornish at Stavka)

For some being cut off behind enemy lines was not a new experience. As well as Eighth Army, the ever unfortunate Second Shock Army was also inside the German net. Here a well-hidden scout of 327th Rifle Division, armed with grenade and PPSh 41 sub-machine gun, watches and waits. With a seventy-one-round drum magazine, the PPSh was an excellent weapon, perfect for forest fighting where volume of fire often counted for more than accuracy. The scout platoons were elite infantrymen used to operating independently. (Courtesy of the Central Museum of the Armed Forces Moscow via Nik Cornish)

For the great majority of the newly arrived men of Eleventh Army the terrain in the Leningrad theatre was in stark contrast to the balmier climes of the Crimean front. Here men of 28th Light Division pick their way through a swamp, more concerned for their footing than for the likelihood of an ambush. They first faced 24th Guards Rifle Division, the lead unit in the Siniavino salient. (Nik Cornish at Stavka)

The defenders of Leningrad had made the city into a fortress in the twelve months since the siege began. The city was criss-crossed by canals and large, stone buildings. The poster reads 'blood for blood, death for death'. (From the fonds of the RGAKFD at Krasnogorsk via Nik Cornish)

The apprehensive looks on these POWs' faces are unsurprising as German propaganda placed much stress on the likely fate of those captured by the Soviets. (Courtesy of the Central Museum of the Armed Forces Moscow via Nik Cornish)

The comparative tranquillity that followed the summer fighting around Leningrad provided a degree of respite for the soldiers and civilians in the city. Here an anti-aircraft gun crew, in full dress uniform, host a visiting delegation of workers from Tajikistan. This Soviet republic was a long way from the epicentre of the war, far to the east on the border with China and Afghanistan. The meeting is taking place on Decembrist Square near St Isaac's Cathedral, seen in the background. (From the fonds of the RGAKFD at Krasnogorsk via Nik Cornish)

And still the digging went on. There was no letting up on the extension and maintenance of Leningrad's defences. (Courtesy of the Central Museum of the Armed Forces Moscow via Nik Cornish)

Chapter Six

Iskra – Operation Spark

The departure of von Manstein in November 1942 meant the postponement of Operation Northern Lights indefinitely. However, it did restore full control of AGN to Kuchler, who would now conduct the siege with Eighteenth Army supported on its right flank by Sixteenth Army, which held the line from near Lake Ilmen south to the junction with Army Group Centre. From the Oranienbaum bridgehead to Pushkin the four divisions of I Army Corps held the line, while to its right LIV Army Corps covered the sector from Pushkin to Annenskoe opposite the city on the Neva River. From there to Shlisselburg XXVI Army Corps was well dug in facing the Neva to its mouth on Lake Ladoga. A further six more divisions filled in as far as Kirishi on the Volkhov River to the south-east. The remaining defences along the Volkhov River to Lake Ilmen were manned by six more infantry divisions that formed XXVIII and XXXVIII army corps. Kuchler's strongest forces held the substantial defence system between Shlisselburg and the Siniavino Heights. The reduction of forces, however, had made Kuchler hold few reserves, which comprised part of 5th Mountain and 96th Infantry divisions. Reinforcements of a kind were on their way in the shape of several Luftwaffe field divisions, but their usefulness was questionable.

On the other side of the Volkhov and Neva rivers sat an increasingly confident Red Army. Continual good news from the Stalingrad region had boosted the confidence of Stalin and Stavka as well as their ambitions. Consequently, plans were rapidly prepared for a significant operation in the Leningrad theatre that would coincide with similar offensives towards the Dnepr River and the Black Sea littoral in the south. The forces available were the Coastal Operational Group in the Oranienbaum bridgehead, the Forty-Second and Fifty-Fifth armies protecting the south and south-eastern sections of the city, from Uritsk–Pushkin–Kolpino to the Neva River. Here the Sixty-Seventh Army (formerly the Neva Operational Group) defended the banks of the river as far as Shlisselburg. To the east the line from Lipki on Lake Ladoga to Lake Ilmen, a distance of over 300km, was the responsibility of the four armies that made up the Volkhov Front. Eighth Army held the right flank resting on the shores of Lake Ladoga followed by Fifty-Fourth, Fourth, Fifty-Ninth and Fifty-Second armies. Second Shock Army was in the rear being reinforced for offensive operations.

Govorov, commanding Leningrad Front, had plans to restore a single defensive zone south and west of the city, re-establishing land contact with the Oranienbaum bridgehead and so driving the siege guns out of range of the city.

His second plan was to breach German lines around Shlisselburg and restore the land link with Volkhov Front, thus breaking AGN's Blockade. The latter plan was accepted by Stavka on 2 December and dubbed Operation Spark (Iskra). Second Shock Army from the east would meet up with Sixty-Seventh Army from the west. The timing of the attack from Leningrad depended on the Neva River being frozen solidly enough to support the weight of light tanks. The first stage of Operation Spark was to break the Blockade, the second involved a push to the south-west to expand this area as far as the Moiska River north of Mga. Both Volkhov and Leningrad fronts were to begin operations on 12 January.

In support of Leningrad Front were over 1,800 guns and mortars which would provide a 2½-hour barrage. The artillery would include batteries that were assigned specific targets such as ammunition or supply dumps. Meretskov had more guns, therefore his front's artillery preparation time would be shorter, less than 1½ hours for Second Shock Army, marginally more for Eighth Army. Air support was in place for both fronts with the focus on ground support. Due to the terrain armoured forces would conduct infantry support missions. Particular attention was paid to providing a powerful engineer presence to overcome the lack of infrastructure and to help destroy German strongpoints. Significant time had been spent on long periods of assault training against replicas of the German positions. Naturally, the Soviets deployed the full array of their *maskirova* techniques to camouflage their preparations. Troops and guns moved at night into vast, hidden dugouts where they waited in the stinking, damp fug for the order to take up their attack positions. When Zhukov arrived in Leningrad late in the night of 11 January even his normally taciturn nature must have been lifted by the sophistication of the build-up.

As the echoes of a final fanfare of Katyusha rockets crashed into the dazed German infantry along the banks of the Neva River the men of Sixty-Seventh Army charged across the frozen waters. As they reached within 50m of the enemy trenches they let out a full throated battle cry, 'Uurah!'

Three infantry divisions broke through the German line on a 3km front between Gorodok and Marino. What remained of the defenders fell back, relentlessly pursued by a Soviet creeping barrage. As the winter sun faded, engineers struggled in the freezing Neva to construct bridges that were able to support heavy tanks, which were to help expand the bridgehead that now measured some 5km wide by 3km deep.

On the Volkhov Front success had rewarded sound preparation. The German line had been penetrated at several points notably around Worker's Settlement 8, Lipki and Kruglaia grove, the latter a key position covering the approaches to Siniavino Heights. Although less impressive than the crossing of the Neva River, it was nonetheless a good start.

XXVI Army Corps reacted quickly rushing men from 96th Infantry and 5th Mountain divisions in to shore up the line. Secondary defences were based around

Soviet villages known as Worker's Settlements (WS), which were generally numbered. These points lay on the few good roads in the area, usually at junctions or overlooking them, consequently they were of immense tactical value. Resistance now focused on these locations. When the weather changed from clear to dull and snowy on 13 January, Volkhov Front slogged on. Second Shock Army had almost encircled Lipki, almost reaching the shore of Lake Ladoga, with penetrations of 8km and 3km. To the west WS 5 was within 2km of the leading units of 136th Infantry division and 61st Tank Brigade that had turned the flank of AGN's hard-fighting 96th Infantry Division. Furthermore, WS 3 and a nearby hill position, key to the defence of Shlisselburg, were under threat. Again, though, dogged German defence slowed down the advance. But at Gorodok 96th Infantry Division with 502nd Heavy Tank Battalion launched a counter attack that resulted in 268th Infantry Division routing back over 2km, a significant distance on such a confined battlefield. The arrival of elements of 5th Mountain Division added weight to this move. Equally useful was the defence of WS 7 covering the approaches to Siniavino.

Recognizing that it was vital to destroy the Neva bridgehead, Kuchler ordered troops in to crush it. As the line facing Volkhov Front was holding relatively firmly reserves could be committed.

Infantry from the 4th SS Division Polizei, as well as two regiments from 61st Infantry Division, were earmarked for the task. As the Germans regrouped for the counter attack fighting raged around WS 8 and reinforcements poured across the Neva bridges as fast as possible heading in the direction of Shlisselburg. WS 7 and 8 held out as the gap between the Soviet troops diminished but the latter was abandoned due to lack of ammunition and the survivors slipped through the lines of Second Shock Army en route for Siniavino. The planned German counter attack was unable to achieve anything but a containment of the bridgehead's southern flank and the Tigers were assigned to support the Shlisselburg sector. On 16 January Soviet 86th Infantry Division reached the suburbs of Shlisselburg, and the following day WS 3 was liberated cutting off the 227th Infantry Division, which formed the bulk of Shlisselburg's garrison and were responsible for the shoreline of Lake Ladoga. Simultaneously, units of the Leningrad Front approached WS 5 from the west.

There was no question of a relief mission to relieve Shlisselburg; its liberation was merely a matter of time, as AGN lacked sufficient strength. Indeed, the strongest part of Kuchler's armour was now trapped there and fuel was running low for the thirsty Tigers. Pressure was also being exerted elsewhere so the mountain and police formations were diverted to more urgent, less hopeless areas such as Siniavino. The troops in Shlisselburg were almost being written off. However, refusing to accept the inevitable, the garrison and other disparate formations banded together and formed Battle Group Huhner (named for its commander), determined to fight its way out. Fighting a series of rearguard action and losing several Tigers on the way, Huhner's command of roughly 8,000 men reached Siniavino on 20 January.

The fall of Shlisselburg on 18 January marked the end of the Blockade. In accordance with the plan both Soviet fronts realigned to expand the liberated zone to the south-west but, having battered vainly against the new German defence line, were forced to call a halt. It had been an incredible week.

In September 1942 it was decided to rotate females in the armed forces so that they served a maximum of twelve months in one location. This action was necessary due to the decline in morale of females on the Eastern Front. (Nik Cornish at Stavka)

Sniping was regarded as an art in the Red Army and the most successful exponents of this art were elevated to heroic status. Both snipers seen here are armed with Mosin-Nagant 7.62mm rifles. By late 1942 it had become politically acceptable to praise the individual as well as the collective effort. (From the fonds of the RGAKFD at Krasnogorsk via Nik Cornish)

Formed in October 1942 from excess air-force personnel, the Luftwaffe field divisions were the brainchild of Herman Goring. Here men of the newly raised 10th Luftwaffe Field Division move into position watching over the Oranienbaum bridgehead in November 1942. 1st Luftwaffe Field Division replaced the 250th Infantry Division north of Lake Ilmen at much the same time. They were well equipped and dressed but virtually untrained for infantry combat. (Nik Cornish at Stavka)

Tank Desant men travel forward mounted on KV-1 tanks during a training exercise with Second Shock Army. What such replacements thought about being assigned to the third rebuilding of this unfortunate force can only be imagined. The Desant troops were carried into action on the tanks holding on to anything they could at speeds of up to 25km per hour. Having survived the ride the men were then expected to go into combat. (Courtesy of the Central Museum of the Armed Forces Moscow via Nik Cornish)

It was vital to coordinate artillery fire from the Volkhov and Leningrad fronts as the distance between the attacking groups was less than 15km. The range of this 280mm BR-5 howitzer was almost 11km. Its tracked chassis was not motorized but it was a towed mortar under Soviet classification. An experienced crew was capable of firing one 200kg round every two minutes. Such an open position suggests a remarkable faith in the local air defences. Care also had to be taken not to break the ice on the Neva River. (From the fonds of the RGAKFD at Krasnogorsk via Nik Cornish)

German bunkers such as this and stronger were a common feature of the defences erected and improved by AGN's engineer battalions during the quiet months of 1942. It was impossible to dig too deeply as the water table in the region was near to the surface, therefore every plot of raised ground was valuable and exploited to the limit. By working around the clock and utilizing forced labour a network of corduroy roads enabled speedy reinforcement of threatened points. (Nik Cornish at Stavka)

Light tanks, such as these T-60 machines, were able to cross the Neva ice at midday on 12 January when Leningrad Front began Operation Spark. The crossing was made with few casualties. The main armament in the turret was a TNSh 20mm gun operated by the commander of this two-man crewed vehicle. With a speed of 44km per hour, they would have proved a difficult target on a smoke-covered battlefield. On average the distance across the river was some 600m. (From the fonds of the RGAKFD at Krasnogorsk via Nik Cornish)

Reserves moving up to support 170th Infantry Division near Gorodok. Despite strong attacks by two infantry brigades with armoured support the defences held. Nowhere on the order of battle of AGN was there a panzer division to counter the threat from Soviet tanks. (Nik Cornish at Stavka)

The lack of a panzer division was offset by the terrain and the presence of 502nd Heavy Tank Battalion with its complement of Tiger Is, which were to prove very useful during the course of the Soviet offensive. As well as nine Tigers, the battalion also included 14 Panzer IIIs. Roughly half of the Panzer IIIs were armed with the 50mm gun, the remainder with the short 75mm gun which also packed an effective punch. (Nik Cornish at Stavka)

One of the stoutest defence positions was centred on the Gorodok power station and hospital on the Neva River. Well-entrenched German machine gunners, some of which had been issued with the new MG 42, of the 399th Grenadier Regiment mowed down wave after wave of 45th Guards Rifle Division. Gorodok held firm, anchoring the German left flank on the Neva River. (Nik Cornish at Stavka)

A KV-1 tank, probably part of 32nd Tank Brigade that took part in the capture of Kruglaia grove on 12 January. A German counter attack recaptured this vital position twenty-four hours later. Over the next few days see-saw fighting reduced the grove to twigs and stumps. Another vital point of the German defensive system it held out to anchor the eastern end of the line where it dominated one of the hard ground routes through an area of swamp. (Nik Cornish at Stavka)

During the fighting around Gorodok power station the Tigers and Panzer IIIs of Heavy Tank Battalion 502 destroyed a dozen T-34s of Sixty-Seventh Army. This one has been recovered virtually intact. However, on 18 January, the Soviets captured a Tiger I before its crew was able to set off the integral demolition charges. Towed out of a marsh, the Tiger was immediately sent to the rear for technical analysis. (Nik Cornish at Stavka)

Although promoted to Marshal of the Soviet Union on 1 January, Zhukov is seen here in his general's uniform. Having arrived at Leningrad Front's HQ on the day Operation Spark began he continually demanded greater efforts from the local commanders. His temper was legendary as was his apparent disregard for human life; however, he did achieve results. Zhukov is waiting for information by a Hughes teleprinter. (Courtesy of the Central Museum of the Armed Forces Moscow via Nik Cornish)

Ski troops such as these were frequently committed when conditions permitted it. 12th Ski Brigade with a force of Marine infantry from 55th Naval Brigade crossed the frozen waters of Lake Ladoga on 14 January, securing a small but important bridgehead between Shlisselburg and Lipki where they pinned part of 227th Infantry Division. (Courtesy of the Central Museum of the Armed Forces Moscow via Nik Cornish)

A mobile German anti-aircraft gun provides cover for a party of troops that have escaped capture during late January 1943. With the loss of Sixth Army at Stalingrad and the lifting of the Leningrad Blockade it was not a happy new year for the Führer or the Reich. (Nik Cornish at Stavka)

Gathering up cast-off arms and equipment became something of a pastime for some civilians in the newly liberated corridor. Such a group, including Red Army supervisors, gather around an abandoned German SdKfz 250 munitions carrier. Without doubt villagers within the liberated zone would also be questioned as to their activities during the occupation in the hunt for collaborators. (Courtesy of the Central Museum of the Armed Forces Moscow via Nik Cornish)

When the men of Leningrad and Volkhov fronts final met up celebration was the order of the day. Here officers from both fronts prepare to celebrate in the ruins of WS 1 mid-morning on 18 January. The officer is Senior Lieutenant Kosav. The 100g daily ration of vodka was doubtless supplemented by locally distilled moonshine. (From the fonds of the RGAKFD at Krasnogorsk via Nik Cornish)

Soviet infantrymen take off in pursuit of German stragglers on the shores of Lake Ladoga. (Courtesy of the Central Museum of the Armed Forces Moscow via Nik Cornish)

As they clear the streets of Leningrad of snow these women can look forward to a better ration of food and drink at the end of their work. Railway construction began almost immediately the Shlisselburg–Lipki corridor was opened. (From the fonds of the RGAKFD at Krasnogorsk via Nik Cornish)

Naturally, the first train that arrived at Leningrad's Finland station was bedecked with pictures of Stalin and slogans extolling the bravery of the people in the face of the fascist aggressors. However trite the words may seem now, it is hard not to agree with the sentiments. The date of arrival was 7 February, less than one month after the commencement of Operation Spark. (From the fonds of the RGAKFD at Krasnogorsk via Nik Cornish)

Chapter Seven

The Air, Sea and Partisan War Over and Around Leningrad

Often overlooked in books such as this are the so-called sideshows. However, to give a reasonably complete picture of the Leningrad siege it is important to include such aspects here, specifically the air, naval and partisan operations that took place in and around the major ground actions.

Naval operations in the Baltic Sea were the responsibility of the Red Banner Baltic Fleet which was under the commanded of Vice Admiral V. F. Tributs, who, somewhat remarkably, retained this position for the duration of the war. In February 1941 the Baltic Fleet had been given a mainly defensive brief should war break out: its major task being the defence of the army's costal flank from Axis seaborne invasion by securing the Gulf of Finland and mining the approaches to its bases. Offensively it was to mine enemy facilities and attack trading vessels and supply routes. Post-war Soviet critiques commented on the limited, vague nature of these instructions. As with much of the preparation for land war, naval matters had been complicated by the absorption of the Baltic States during 1940. The Soviets had gained harbours such as Liepaja, Riga, Tallinn and Hanko in Finland. However, these bases were not fully operational nor, more critically, were their landward defences in a good condition. But in Tributs the Baltic Fleet possessed a commander who was sensible enough to interpret signs of German aggressiveness as just what they were — the prelude to war. Consequently, the Baltic Fleet was put on Readiness State 1, that is fully operational, and Tributs moved his staff to its advanced command post at midnight on 21 June 1941, mere hours before the first shots were fired. Just four hours later the former Latvian steamer, the *Gaisma*, now part of the Soviet merchant fleet, was sunk.

Liepaja was lost to five German torpedo boats on 28 June and Riga several days later. The Baltic Fleet had now assembled much of its strength in the Estonian port of Tallinn. Tributs was ordered to evacuate Tallinn on 26 August and two days later four convoys left the harbour at roughly two-hour intervals. These comprised some 160 vessels, ranging from tankers and coastal patrol boats to the cruiser *Kirov* which Tributs took as his flagship. Thousands of military personnel were distributed between the ships, but alongside them were thousands of passengers who formed part of the pro-Soviet administrations in the Baltic States, as well as civilians being forcibly evacuated to contribute to the Soviet war effort.

During the next twenty-four hours German and Finnish mine fields, submarine attacks and Luftwaffe strikes accounted for 65 ships and some 16,000 casualties. The Germans fished a further 10,000 out of the sea or off the beaches. The remaining vessels, including the heavily damaged *Kirov*, limped into Kronstadt or Leningrad as Hanko was now under siege and its approaches heavily mined.

With their fleet bottled up the Soviets had few effective naval assets to prevent the Kriegsmarine occupying the Estonian Islands, which was done during September and October 1941. With the evacuation of Hanko in early December the Baltic Fleet was effectively reduced to floating artillery, firing in support of the Oranienbaum bridgehead from Kronstadt and the quays along the Neva River to cover the city. Nor was the Kriegsmarine much more active. Mines were laid, Estonian partisans ferried about and submarines patrolled. The situation began to parallel that on the land. Defences such as minefields and anti-submarine nets were laid and increased until virtually no ship of either side ventured into vaguely hostile waters. Such was the effectiveness of Axis anti-submarine warfare that ten out of twenty-one Soviet submarines sent out of Kronstadt in autumn 1941 failed to return. During the spring of 1943 a 97km anti-submarine net was placed across the Gulf of Finland without interference from the Baltic Fleet.

Nevertheless, Stavka did not allow its seamen to rot on floating batteries engaged in what Tributs called 'their duel' with German artillery. Out of Baltic Sea Fleet personnel 9 rifle brigades, over 30 separate battalions, including a ski unit, and 32 artillery batteries, including railway guns, were formed. Indeed, it is arguable that Oranienbaum survived due to the efforts of the sailors and coastal gunners.

Through the efforts of the Ladoga Lake Flotilla the Soviet navy achieved much success in evacuating people and machinery and ferrying in supplies. Furthermore, the defeat of the Axis' Naval Detachment K during 1942 was a battle honour that force could certainly claim.

On 5 November 1943 the Baltic Fleet was tasked with transporting the Second Shock Army along with its equipment across the ice tracks into the Oranienbaum bridgehead. Having kept the pocket supplied and supported for two years it was fitting that the Baltic Fleet should contribute to the final offensive that pushed AGN back into Estonia, away from Kronstadt and Leningrad.

As well as providing ground and sea support the Baltic Fleet also supplied air support. The Baltic Fleet had three regiments of fighters, roughly 180 machines, many of which were obsolete types. The first appearance of the Luftwaffe over the Leningrad Military District was to deliver mines to the Kronstadt approaches on 22 June 1941.

The Soviet air force, properly titled the Red Army Air Forces and known by the acronym VVS, had assigned VII Fighter Corps with over 400 fighters and 180 medium bombers to North Western Front. The ground-based air-defence organization for Leningrad was known as the PVO and disposed of 100 heavy a/a guns over 200 quadruple machine guns, searchlights and barrage balloons.

Unfortunately, the PVO deployed only one radar station and that was experimental. Happily, the Luftwaffe did not seriously trouble the city for several months as it concentrated on first gaining air superiority over the VVS and then on ground support missions.

Army Group North disposed of the smallest air asset, Luftflotte 1 (Colonel General Keller), assigned to Operation Barbarossa. By early September this force had been reduced to roughly 100 fighters and 200 bombers. However, with the arrival of Fliegerkorps VIII's Stukas and ME 110 fighters the balance tipped significantly in the German's favour. Despite the reinforcements released by Stavka, the Soviets were shot out of the sky. By the end of 1941 both air forces were much reduced. Fliegerkorps VIII had left having inflicted heavy damage on the Baltic Fleet's two battleships and sinking two destroyers and other smaller craft. With the onset of winter the Baltic Fleet's shallower draught vessels took shelter along the docks of the Neva River under cover of the PVO a/a guns. As the PVO was now under the direct command of the VVS fire plans and ammunition distribution proceeded more smoothly. The seasonal respite gave the VVS time to rebuild its numbers with Lend Lease aircraft such as the P-40 Tomahawk/Kittyhawk, Hurricanes and domestically produced LaGG-3 fighters.

By the end of January 1942 the VVS, with 230 aircraft, enjoyed a superiority of 2½ : 1 over Luftflotte 1. Although some air raids were carried out over Leningrad, it was not blitzed like London, and the Baltic Fleet and selected factories seem to have been the major targets. When the weather improved in April a major attempt was made to destroy the Soviet capital ships. Some damage was caused but none were sunk. Oddly, no serious efforts were made to disrupt traffic on the 'Road of Life' or Lake Ladoga and by the summer of 1942 Luftflotte 1 was mainly flying ground support missions along the Volkhov River line. Increased a/a capacity and a wider radar net acted as a significant deterrent to bombing missions over the city. Axis demands for air support in other sectors of the Eastern Front led to a reduction in the strength of Luftflotte 1. This led to an upsurge in VVS activity, particularly the use of the IL-2 Shturmovik ground-attack aircraft. Luftwaffe headquarters responded to this increased threat and provided reinforcements which enabled Luftflotte 1 to clear the skies over the battlefield. In part this was due to the arrival of the FW-190 fighter, which was superior to anything in the Soviet inventory. Indeed, during September 1942 Luftflotte 1 claimed 290 kills for the loss of 34 of their own. This sort of destruction is reflected in the tally of one FW-190 ace, Walter Nowotny, who in a 4-month spree shot down 135 VVS machines. But the happy hunting time was drawing to an end by October 1943. Luftflotte 1 counted only 26 fighters against 400 VVS aircraft with an additional 400 bombers and Shturmoviks. No longer were a handful of aces capable of restoring the Luftwaffe's control of the skies over Leningrad. In fact, there were more men in the Luftwaffe field divisions deployed in the siege lines than flying or maintaining the aircraft available.

In many ways the air war reflected the ground war around Leningrad. AGN's efforts to take the city had been held by a combination of desperate, at times suicidal fighting on the one hand and last-gasp thrusts by over-stretched attackers on the other. Successful German defensive operations led to the high command reducing the ground forces in the area, placing increased reliance on positional warfare with small-scale counter attacks. However, as the experience and quality of the Soviets grew in line with their strength and numbers such a strategy could, in the long run, only fail.

Almost wiping out the VVS was not enough, nor was almost sinking battleships and supply barges. Nor indeed was it enough to almost pacify the civilians who lived behind AGN's lines as they would also prove to be a growing strain of poison in the German supply system. The partisan movement in the Leningrad and surrounding regions had been activated during the first days of Operation Barbarossa and would grow over the course of the next two years into a force to be taken seriously by the security forces attached to AGN.

Although during the Russian Civil War the Red Army had made use of partisan formations, not until the mid-1930s had their value in wartime been acknowledged. However, a change in military doctrine that all future wars would be fought on enemy soil led to partisan operations falling into disfavour. Nevertheless, the speed of the German advance prompted various, initially unofficial, partisan movements to appear. As AGN spread across the Baltic States towards Leningrad it passed through territories that were not ethnically Russian or pro-communist, and consequently few Balts were prepared to take up clandestine arms against forces they regarded as liberators. The speed of the German advance led to the isolation of thousands of Red Army personnel of all ranks who often decided to fight on in a partisan capacity until such time as they could cross the lines and rejoin their own side. The three security divisions at the disposal of AGN were composed of old, often unfit men officered by pensioners from the Kaiser's army: consequently, they proved to be ill-suited for the type of warfare that they were committed to. But in their wake came the men of SS Einsatzgruppen A who were to implement Hitler's racial-political theories by exterminating Jews and communists. However, in a very short time these agents of genocide found themselves engaged with a more formidable foe than children and the aged as the *untermensch* of the east fought back.

One of the few achievements of Voroshilov's brief time in Leningrad was, in tandem with the Leningrad Party Committee, to form the nucleus of a partisan movement which Stalin had officially encouraged in his speech of early July. Selection for partisans was rigorous. Each candidate had to have an unimpeachable party record, be physically fit and preferably have experience with firearms. By September 1941 over 200 groups each of roughly 40 had been inserted behind AGN's lines. Unsurprisingly, thirteen of these units had been recruited from the Leningrad Institute of Physical Culture.

On 27 September a partisan headquarters was established under the leadership of M. N. Nikitin, secretary of the Leningrad Regional Committee. Its main task was to coordinate partisan and regular forces cooperation. But as well as attacking enemy troops and gathering information, possibly the partisans more crucial mission was to re-establish the Party's power and influence in the 'Temporarily Occupied Territories', as the German-held provinces were known. In this latter task the Second Partisan Brigade excelled, establishing an autonomous partisan *krai* (a Soviet administrative district) between Dno, Kholm and Staraia Russa. Despite the efforts of the security troops and the Einsatzgruppen, the *krai* flourished, re-opening schools, medical centres and collective farms. The brutally repressive counter measures undertaken by the Germans only increased sympathy for the partisans. The Dno *krai* remained in existence for almost twelve months until crushed during Operation Karlsbad. Despite this setback, the Leningrad Partisan HQ recruited further groups and during 1943 took part in Operation Rail War that summer. Operation Rail War was designed to cause chaos along the Axis' railway supply lines during and after Operation Citadel and to coincide with Leningrad and Volkhov front's offensive against the Mga salient. As the regular forces scaled down their efforts those of the partisans increased. With the announcement of conscription and evacuation of Soviet civilians to work on the Panther Line and in German industry many people took to the marshes and forests. When the Siniavino Heights were lost by the Germans partisan groups began to attack more generally, with the intention of raising rebellion behind AGN now that it was clear that it was falling back from its siege lines. In early November 1943 word went out from Leningrad ordering the partisans to step up their intelligence-gathering operations and to prepare to carry out diversionary attacks on road and rail links. When the final offensive to push AGN back into Estonia began in January 1944 the partisans contributed once again, cutting telegraph lines, derailing trains and rounding up German stragglers. Finally, in March 1944 the Partisan HQ was dissolved as the fighting had moved off Soviet territory and the majority of partisans had joined the Red Army or been assigned duties elsewhere.

The symbol of Bolshevik naval power, the cruiser *Aurora* at her mooring in Oranienbaum. The *Aurora* was bombed on 30 September 1941 and sank aground. To the foreground is one of the PVO's 85mm anti-aircraft guns. (From the fonds of the RGAKFD at Krasnogorsk via Nik Cornish)

Soviet naval anti-aircraft gunners aboard a vessel in Kronstadt harbour. The main island, Kotlin, on which Kronstadt stands formed part of a chain of fortified islands that covered the sea approach to Leningrad. The waters around it were frozen from early December to April each year. (From the fonds of the RGAKFD at Krasnogorsk via Nik Cornish)

The Baltic Fleet deployed over 125,000 men to fight onshore. They were organized into nine rifle brigades. The Fourth Rifle Brigade defended the 'Road of Life' across Lake Ladoga. When in the front line the sailors wore infantry uniform. Patrols such as this were a common sight along all coastal and lakeside pathways. (From the fonds of the RGAKFD at Krasnogorsk via Nik Cornish)

A Kriegsmarine patrol ship cruises the Baltic Sea. Judging by the rating's sleepy demeanour it is proving to be a quiet day. (Nik Cornish at Stavka)

A pilot and a member of his ground crew discuss maintenance. (Nik Cornish at Stavka)

The crew of a Tupolev SB-2 poses for the camera during the early spring of 1942. SB translates as 'high-speed bomber', for which task, though generally at night, it was used around Leningrad. (Courtesy of the Central Museum of the Armed Forces Moscow via Nik Cornish)

A quadruple 7.62mm a/a machine gun mounting fires, illuminating the silhouette of St Isaac's Cathedral. Such weapons were often integrated with conventional a/a gun batteries to provide cover against low-flying enemy aircraft on strafing runs. (From the fonds of the RGAKFD at Krasnogorsk via Nik Cornish)

An early Il-2 Shturmovik brought down behind German lines is disassembled to be studied. This early, single-seat version was vulnerable to German fighters due to the weight of its armoured cockpit and relatively slow speed. (Nik Cornish at Stavka)

Repairing a Stuka that had overshot the runway during the summer of 1942. (Nik Cornish at Stavka)

The presentation parade for a P-39 Airacobra regiment, part of VII Fighter Corps PVO, that has just received Guards status. Senior officers are in uniform, others in coveralls. The men's position is traditional, as is the position of the propellers. (Courtesy of TASS via Nik Cornish)

A Latvian police volunteer unit seen here with its German police officers. Thousands of Estonians and Latvians enrolled in such units during the course of the war. Their antipathy to the Soviet regime did much to contain the spread of anti-German partisan groups into the Baltic States. (Nik Cornish at Stavka)

A Red Army officer is interrogated by members of AGN's intelligence branch. The appalling treatment meted out to Soviet POWs was witnessed by Soviet civilians during the first winter of the war and increased their hatred of the invaders and led to their support for the partisans. (Nik Cornish at Stavka)

Mounted partisans patrol the perimeter of the *krai* in spring 1942. Partisan leaders insisted on tight, semi-military discipline with even swearing forbidden. Prospective recruits had to serve a probationary term and their every word and mannerism was observed lest they prove to be an informer. (Courtesy of the Central Museum of the Armed Forces Moscow via Nik Cornish)

The terrain behind the lines of AGN was ideal to wage partisan warfare. Thousands of square kilometres of almost uninhabited swamp, marshland and forest allowed the partisans to fade away from their pursuers, who found it increasingly difficult to exercise more than token control over the rural population. (Courtesy of the Central Museum of the Armed Forces Moscow via Nik Cornish)

Public floggings such as the one seen here were one way in which the occupation administration sought to crush the smuggling of foodstuffs into Leningrad. The smuggler's bag is exposed to the camera. (From the fonds of the RGAKFD at Krasnogorsk via Nik Cornish)

The consequences of being a partisan or merely suspected of harbouring partisans was sufficient to merit execution at the hands of the security forces. The partisan war was merciless; no quarter was expected nor any given. (From the fonds of the RGAKFD at Krasnogorsk via Nik Cornish)

Conscripted labour to work on the Panther Line. Hundreds of such people were freed by the partisans and they in turn rounded against the occupation forces. (Nik Cornish at Stavka)

In mid-1942 AGN suggested to Berlin that men of the Replacement Army complete their training by supporting security formations with anti-partisan sweeps. The idea was taken up. Conditions in summer 1942 are evident here. Although partisan operations were not as widespread behind AGN as in other areas, the possibility of such activities was sufficient to send a shiver down the spine of many a German soldier on guard duty or riding with a supply convoy through the forests. (Nik Cornish at Stavka)

Partisan work at its simplest. (Courtesy of the Central Museum of the Armed Forces Moscow via Nik Cornish)

A collaborator is given summary justice by members of Fifth Leningrad Partisan Brigade during January 1944. Rarely were known 'enemies of the people' given the benefit of a trial. (Courtesy of the Central Museum of the Armed Forces Moscow via Nik Cornish)

Chapter Eight

Polar Star to Panther Line

It may have been an incredible week but before the celebrations in Leningrad and Moscow were over Stalin, Stavka and Zhukov were planning nothing less than the destruction of AGN and the removal of any further threat to the city. Under the codename of Operation Polar Star, North Western Front, supported by Leningrad and Volkhov fronts, would envelop Sixteenth, Seventeenth and Eighteenth armies and dwarf the *kessel* (cauldron) in which Germany's Sixth Army was choking in its death throes far to the south in Stalingrad.

Although only playing supporting roles, Leningrad and Volkhov fronts would begin their attacks on 8 February. The objective was to draw off AGN's reserves one week before North Western Front began its elimination of the Demiansk pocket in Sixteenth Army's sector, before racing off to complete the encirclement of AGN via Staraia Russia, Luga and finally Narva.

Leningrad and Volkhov fronts were to execute a pincer movement. Leningrad Front's Fifty-Fifth Army would break through German lines at Krasny Bor; simultaneously, Volkhov Front's Fifty-Fourth Army would attack north-westwards towards Tosno, where both fronts would link up. At that point both fronts would expand the land bridge to Leningrad and wheel to the south west splitting Sixteenth and Eighteenth armies. To prevent Eighteenth Army shuffling men from the Siniavino Heights area Sixty-Seventh and Second Shock armies were ordered to carry out diversionary attacks. To exploit the anticipated German disarray winter mobile troops, such as cavalry, aerosans and ski troops, would be unleashed into Kuchler's rear as North Western Front advanced to administer the coup de grâce.

Less than a week after the last emaciated, lice-infested diehards at Stalingrad had surrendered Leningrad and Volkhov fronts began their attacks. Defending the Krasny Bor sector, some 32km long, were the 250th Spanish Infantry and 4th SS Polizei divisions: hammered by a two-hour artillery bombardment, their morale was so shaken that the attacks of two Soviet rifle divisions broke through their positions to liberate Krasny Bor some 5km behind the lines on 10 February. It was an auspicious beginning.

However, Volkhov Front's Fifty-Fourth Army ran into firmer resistance. Four rifle divisions supported by a tank brigade took two days to achieve a slightly smaller dent in 96th Infantry Division's defence system. This sterling defence against Volkhov Front allowed Kuchler to commit a Tiger platoon to Krasny Bor.

On 12 February Sixty-Seventh and Second Shock armies began their offensive against the Siniavino Heights and the salient that ended at Gorodok on the Neva

River, some 10km from Shlisselburg. It took six days of vicious fighting to take Gorodok but, despite denuding their forces at Siniavino, Eighteenth Army retained the high ground and within a week the Soviet attacks ground to a halt. The tenacity of the defenders, the exhaustion of the attackers and an unforeseen thaw combined in the Germans favour. Other than the loss of Krasny Bor, the lines around Leningrad remained intact. Now it fell to North Western Front to deliver the main attack in pursuit of the hoped for encirclement of AGN.

Soviet intelligence alerted Moscow to German preparations to withdraw from Demiansk, and therefore Zhukov ordered North Western Front to attack. From 15–27 February Twenty-Seventh and First Shock armies hurled themselves time and again against the German lines only to be rebuffed by well-entrenched veteran infantry. Even 30,000 casualties gained Stalin precious little and the offensive was halted for a week. The Germans successfully completed the evacuation of Demiansk on 19 February, thus reducing Sixteenth Army's front in the area significantly. Forces released were transferred to cover Novgorod. There was to be no grand sweep to Narva from below Lake Ilmen, North Western Front had failed and now attention focused on the activities of Leningrad and Volkhov fronts.

Leningrad and Volkhov fronts were allowed until 14 March before they were instructed to begin again, but on a reduced scale, concentrating on Mga and Siniavino with a link-up point south-west of Mga at Voitolovo. North Western Front was to provide the diversionary attacks around Novgorod, Eighth Army from Volkhov Front and Fifty-Fifth Army from Leningrad Front would be the pincers.

Once again the battered infantrymen of Second Shock Army would drag themselves out of the trench lines and hurl themselves at the Siniavino Heights, but only if developments elsewhere proved favourable.

On 5 March the diversionary attacks began and immediately foundered against the German strongpoints, heavily reinforced with infantry released from the Demiansk pocket. Now Eighteenth Army could concentrate on its own front.

Events further south, around Kharkov, forced Stavka to weaken North Western Front and reduce the scope of Operation Polar Star to the reduction of the Mga salient and the liberation of Staraia Russa.

Leningrad Front opened its attack around Krasny Bor on 19 March and once again achieved early success, penetrating 3km into the lines of the SS Polizei Division. However, a counter attack by the SS Flanders Legion and 502nd Heavy Tank Battalion's Tigers drove the Soviets back to their start line twenty-four hours later. To the east Volkhov Front had fared somewhat better, slicing a 28sq km gash in the German lines at the point where the 1st and 223rd Infantry divisions connected. Reinforcements from four other divisions were rushed to seal the breakthrough, which they succeeded in doing. Although both Soviet fronts attempted further attacks as March drew on, nothing of significance was accomplished. With the onset of the thaw and the consequent quagmire of the *rasputitsa* Operation Polar Star was finally halted.

Having recovered his equilibrium following the Stalingrad catastrophe Hitler now turned his mind to the upcoming summer offensive. Keeping alive the prospect of taking Leningrad by reviving operations Northern Lights and Moor Fire, AGN proposed Operation Parkplatz which would advance the siege lines to Shlisselburg and Lipki, thereby cutting off the city's land bridge, and following this a direct assault would follow. With his attention focused on the Kursk offensive, Hitler agreed to release the requisite forces when Operation Citadel had succeeded. However, with Citadel an obvious failure by mid-July 1943, Operation Parkplatz was consigned to oblivion. It was left to Stalin to order Leningrad and Volkhov fronts over to the offensive on the blood-soaked Mga–Siniavino axis.

The dual purpose of this operation was to reduce the artillery fire on the newly built railway line, but more significantly to prepare the ground for the raising of the siege later in the year. Unsurprisingly, the Soviets would employ another pincer movement: Leningrad Front's Fifty-Fifth Army would attempt yet again to link up with Volkhov Front's Eighth Army near Mga, whilst the former's Sixty-Seventh Army battered at the Siniavino fortifications.

Sixty-Seventh and Eighth armies began their attack shortly after dawn on 22 July. Sixty-Seventh Army, commanded by Dukhanov, made a slight impression in the wake of a ninety-minute bombardment, but the bodies of Soviet riflemen soon carpeted the slopes of Siniavino in a ghastly re-enactment of the British experience during the first day of the Battle of the Somme. Comfortably entrenched German machine gunners harvested a rich crop during those long summer days. Soviet tanks proved equally simple prey for the Tigers as the T-34s tried to provide respite for their infantry. After four weeks on 22 August Stavka reduced the scale of the offensive. This time the capture of the Siniavino Heights was the objective to which end both fronts bent their efforts. A frontal attack was launched with massive air and artillery support. Troops of Eighth Army hit the eastern end of the German position as three divisions of XXX Guard Rifle Corps took the more direct approach. A more subtle fire plan provided the element of surprise that took the Germans unawares, and the guardsmen finally raised the red flag over the Siniavino Heights on 15 September 1943.

Kuchler reorganized his defences and, with Hitler's authorization, shortened the line thus freeing some four divisions. The Führer also granted permission to begin work on an immense defensive network – the Panther Line – which would run from Narva through Pskov to Ostrov where Army Group North abutted Army Group Centre. Deep in the rear of AGN the Panther Line represented tacit German acceptance that, barring a miracle, Leningrad was now an objective beyond their grasp. For the men of Sixteenth and Eighteenth armies it was simply a matter of waiting for the inevitable Soviet winter offensive. The autumn of 1943 was for both sides a time of patient anticipation.

When the rail line through the Shlisselburg gap opened it was under shell fire almost every day. The railway workers named this section of the line 'the corridor of death'. With a range of almost 15km against ground targets this 88mm flak gun was capable of hitting targets within the corridor. (Nik Cornish at Stavka)

Well camouflaged for the season men of the Spanish division near Krasny Bor move to take up their positions. They sustained over 3,000 casualties. However, Kuchler, commander of AGN, had lost faith in the Spaniards and asked that they be withdrawn. The Blue Division remained with AGN until October 1943 when it was withdrawn at Franco's request. (Nik Cornish at Stavka)

A German courier rides across a relatively open tract of land in the rear of AGN. Such *Meldereiter* were not an uncommon sight when conditions were difficult for vehicles or fuel was short. This photograph was taken on 3 February 1943. (Nik Cornish at Stavka)

Mortar teams give fire support to the diversionary attacks mounted by Sixty-Seventh Army during February 1943. This appears to be an 82mm weapon firing at close to its maximum elevation of 80 degrees, suggesting a target that is very close by. (Courtesy of the Central Museum of the Armed Forces Moscow via Nik Cornish)

A German anti-tank unit manhandles a 75mm PAK 97/38 into position. A conversion of the famous French 75 of First World War vintage, it was a highly effective addition to the anti-tank capability of the German infantry. It was with such a gun that a Dutchman won the first Knight's Cross awarded to a non-German for knocking out nineteen T-34s of Soviet 124th Tank Brigade of Fifty-Fifth Army in mid-February. (Nik Cornish at Stavka)

A T-34/76 noses its way through a copse of evergreens before attacking the SS Polizei Division lines. A total of thirty were destroyed in short order by Tigers of 502nd Heavy Tank Battalion. In terrain such as this the speed and manoeuvrability of the T-34 was almost useless. (Courtesy of the Central Museum of the Armed Forces Moscow via Nik Cornish)

A Soviet 25mm anti-aircraft gun keeps watch for Luftwaffe activity. During this period air support was limited by the weather. (Courtesy of the Central Museum of the Armed Forces Moscow via Nik Cornish)

The front line from the Soviet side. (Courtesy of the Central Museum of the Armed Forces Moscow via Nik Cornish)

Gathering up surplus equipment and transporting it was a necessary task following a successful defensive action for the men of AGN. Here a warmly clad landser sits on a Finnish style *akjas* sledge. (Nik Cornish at Stavka)

An mg 34 team of 1st Luftwaffe Field Division pose in their battered position. This unit was attacked by elements of Fifty-Second Army during the last two weeks of March. It was unfortunate for these men that it was decreed that they retain their Luftwaffe uniforms. Consequently, the Soviets targeted these units for attack as their fighting capabilities were know to be inferior to their army colleagues. (Nik Cornish at Stavka)

The coming of the thaw led to the muddy season which even affected the wide-tracked armoured vehicles of the Red Army. The KV-1 tank to the front is about to attempt to pull the forward T-34 out of the mire. (Courtesy of the Central Museum of the Armed Forces Moscow via Nik Cornish)

Female snipers are congratulated by a senior officer on their return from a successful mission. Both ladies are wearing the two-piece camouflage suit. Many such women who served in the army had been recruited from members of pre-war rifle clubs. (Courtesy of the Central Museum of the Armed Forces Moscow via Nik Cornish)

The commander of a heavily camouflaged Tiger of 502nd Heavy Tank Battalion watches flak bursts around a Soviet air attack. (Nik Cornish at Stavka)

The German lines from the air presented a moonscape of craters. The group of IL-2 Shturmovik ground-attack aircraft appear to be the early single-seat version. The more familiar two-seater was introduced to front-line service in August 1943. (Courtesy of the Central Museum of the Armed Forces Moscow via Nik Cornish)

A Soviet artillery major watches the effect of his unit's fire on the Siniavino lines. The highest point of the German lines was 164m. The position was taken when the Soviet gunners reverted to their 1916 tactics of a creeping barrage instead of the usual torrent of fire. (From the fonds of the RGAKFD at Krasnogorsk via Nik Cornish)

Reading a letter from friends or family, two Soviet riflemen pass the nervous time before going over the top. Conditions during the summer campaign season resembled the Western Front during the First World War. (Courtesy of the Central Museum of the Armed Forces Moscow via Nik Cornish)

Officers of 5th Mountain Division watch as their men defend the line during the attacks of Eighth Army. The Soviets deployed a 5 : 1 superiority in men. Reinforcements from 132nd Infantry Division reduced this imbalance somewhat, as did an infusion of the ubiquitous Tigers. (Nik Cornish at Stavka)

During the summer of 1943 the Leningrad region's partisan movement began to fight in earnest. Indeed, there was even talk of a concerted uprising to the rear of AGN. It has been suggested that rumours of this event prompted Hitler's agreement to the construction of and withdrawal to the Panther Line. The image clearly shows the problem of casualty evacuation faced by the partisans in this area. (From the fonds of the RGAKFD at Krasnogorsk via Nik Cornish)

Work begins on the Panther Line utilizing a Soviet-built Stalinets S 65 tractor. (Nik Cornish at Stavka)

Re-positioning the artillery as AGN prepares to face the Soviet winter offensive. A battery of 105mm howitzers are towed westwards under heavy camouflage. (Nik Cornish at Stavka)

Chapter Nine

Return to the Luga River

For the *Frontoviki* patient anticipation may have been the case but at command level planning for the winter offensive began in mid-September 1943, when Govorov and Meretskov outlined their ideas to Stavka. Once again it was a pincer movement and once again it was designed to clear the region west and south of Leningrad and destroy Lindemann's Eighteenth Army.

The first thrust was to come from the heavily reinforced Oranienbaum bridgehead, which would link up with Forty-Second Army attacking out of Leningrad itself near Krasnoe Selo. With this accomplished Sixty-Seventh Army would drive towards Krasnogvardeisk and Forty-Second Army to Kingisepp.

Volkhov Front's Eighth, Fifty-Fourth and Fifty-Ninth armies would attack the right flank of Eighteenth Army above Lake Ilmen and push towards Tosno and Luga, which would entail the liberation of Novgorod. The entire offensive was codenamed Operation Neva.

South of Lake Ilmen Second Baltic Front (formerly Western Front) would conduct diversionary attacks aimed at preventing Sixteenth Army sending reinforcements to its sister formation in AGN.

As the Red Army was furiously pursuing Army Group South out of Ukraine and about to engage in an offensive against Army Group Centre, reinforcements for the Leningrad and Volkhov fronts would be modest. Nevertheless, the Soviets possessed a reasonable superiority in infantry 8 : 5, 4 : 1 in tanks and 2 : 1 in artillery. However, this superiority was somewhat greater than it may have seemed. From mid-October when Franco removed the Spanish 250th Infantry Division OKH (the German High Command) had stripped AGN of its veteran infantry divisions, two of which had left for AGS. As AGN, particularly Eighteenth Army, was preparing several defensive belts including the Rollbahn and Panther lines, three of its infantry divisions and 502nd Heavy Tank Battalion had been transferred to Sixteenth Army. The only armour in Eighteenth Army was that attached to 11th SS Panzer Grenadier Division Nordland and 4th SS Panzer Grenadier Brigade Nederland, which was deployed covering the Oranienbaum bridgehead in support of 9th and 10th Luftwaffe field divisions. The six divisions of L and LIV army corps defended the central sector from Uritsk to Tosno, while XXVI Army Corps held Mga with three infantry divisions. The line down to Lake Ilmen was the responsibility of the seven infantry divisions of XXVIII and XXXVIII army corps with only a single infantry division, 61st, in reserve. The major defensive positions centred on towns and communications centres such as Novgorod, Krasnoe Selo, Mga and

Pushkin. Although Kuchler, commander of Army Group North, was aware that his opponents were preparing an offensive, his attitude was sanguine, indeed intelligence had pointed out that reinforcements were being moved into Oranienbaum. However, with the Red Army active elsewhere it was deemed unlikely that operations around Leningrad and along the Volkhov River would prove significantly troublesome. Nevertheless, work proceeded on the Panther Line, which ran from Narva through Pskov to Nevel where it linked up with AGC. Kuchler anticipated retiring to it in a phased manner through a series of positions between January and May 1944. Hitler had agreed to this strategic withdrawal, codenamed Operation Blau, on 22 December, on condition that a major Soviet offensive forced his hand. Until such an event Kuchler was confident that the strength of his defences and the tenacity of his troops would hold out. Unfortunately, for AGN the Soviet *maskirovka* had proved highly effective and when the series of Soviet blows came Kuchler's defensive abilities would be tried to the utmost.

Meretskov, Govorov and Stavka were highly concerned that their offensive would fall on empty lines and had covered themselves with an alternative Operation Neva, number 1, should the Germans pull back. In the event it was Operation Neva 2 that burst over the men of III SS Panzer Corps on 14 January 1944.

At 10.40 hours that morning three divisions of Soviet infantry burst from the smoke, howling their battle cry and hitting the junction of 9th and 10th Luftwaffe field divisions. Overrunning the forward positions within twenty-four hours, the men of Second Shock Army had created a salient of some 70sq km aimed at Ropsha. To the east another bombardment softened up the positions of L Army Corps before the men of Forty-Second Army went into the attack on 15 January. Shrugging off counter attacks from III SS Panzer Corps, Second Shock Army advanced a further 6km as Forty-Second Army ground forward some 8km in two days in the Pulkovo region. Plodding though the Soviet advance now became, the pincers were closing around 126th Infantry and 9th Luftwaffe field divisions, as well as eighty-five pieces of heavy siege artillery that had spent the last two years shelling Leningrad.

Kuchler had, on 17 January, requested permission to withdraw from the Mga salient using the troops released to shore up his creaking lines elsewhere. As OKH debated the matter it provided interim relief by ordering 12th Panzer Division and Heavy Tank Battalion 502 to join Eighteenth Army. As the former was coming from AGC and the latter from Sixteenth Army they had to run the gamut of the increasingly effective partisan attacks, which held up their arrival for several days. The Soviets settled any further German discussion by the simple expedient of pushing through the last defences at Ropsha and closing the pincers on 19 January. Krasnoe Selo, Peterhof and Uritsk had all fallen by 20 January, but as the Soviet infantry were unable to keep pace with their armoured spearheads and seal the perimeter thousands of German troops were able to escape captivity. Less than a week had elapsed and now the Oranienbaum bridgehead and Leningrad Front presented a single line and Eighteenth Army was in full retreat. Faced with this crisis Kuchler, without reference to Hitler, ordered the units defending Mga to pull back. However, it was too late as the Volkhov Front was also on the move against the right flank of Eighteenth Army near Novgorod. The first attack on the city fared badly but a surprise attack across the frozen waters of Lake Ilmen provoked a juggling of XXXVIII Army Corps formations. As a result of increased pressure Fifty-Ninth Army began to advance, creating a gap some 20km deep between XXXVIII and XXVIII army corps. Fifty-Fourth Army attacked in support of this progress but ran into difficulties in a morass of part-frozen swamps and dense woodland. Kuchler requested permission to realign his forces, finally doing so as Hitler prevaricated. Novgorod was evacuated, depopulated and razed to the ground, which fate went some way to assuage Hitler who regarded it as a powerful symbol of Russian history. The Soviet liberators found only fifty civilians in the smoking ruins; the remainder of the population was on its way westwards to labour for the Reich. With both its flanks in the air it was vital for Eighteenth Army to stabilize its position as the northern flank of Sixteenth Army was now in danger.

With Stavka's approval Leningrad and Volkhov fronts now embarked on the next phase of Operation Neva, an offensive to liberate Pushkin, Tosno and Krasnogvardeisk by Leningrad Front and Luga and Lyuban as the objectives for Volkhov Front. Fighting began again on 21 January with Second Shock and Forty-Second armies pushing forward. As the men of Eighteenth Army tumbled into the defences of the Rollbahn Line they were pursued by Soviets determined to give them no respite. While Govorov berated his commanders for their tardiness, his front's casualties mounted in the face of well-directed defensive operations and counter attacks. Despite the best efforts of the Germans Mga fell, but elsewhere success eluded Leningrad Front until 26 January when Krasnogvardeisk was liberated. On the same day Sixty-Seventh Army took Tosno and the western end of the Rollbahn Line began to crumble, and twenty-four hours later Lyuban was in Soviet hands. Now the road to Luga and Kingisepp was beginning to clear. Volkhov Front also began to threaten Luga and Kuchler noted that his armies had lost touch with each other. To rectify matters elements of 8th Jaeger, 280th Infantry and 1st Luftwaffe field divisions, plus a brigade of cavalry, were formed into two combat groups to maintain the armies' flank connection – and they just succeeded. Indeed, the stiffening of Eighteenth Army's defences coincided with a faltering of Leningrad Front's impetus. Nor were Volkhov or Second Baltic fronts faring any better. Resupply of ammunition, food and fuel was falling to critical lows due to German engineers' destruction of the infrastructure, sowing of mines and booby traps and the changeable weather, with frost alternating with thaw.

Although Eighteenth Army had fallen back over 100km it was still capable of defending its shortened lines. To its right Sixteenth Army had also withdrawn and it too was still in the fight. As they took up positions in the Panther Line, the men of Eighteenth Army paused to lick their wounds. Across no-man's-land the Soviets had achieved their primary objective of clearing the Leningrad district and driving the Germans back to the west. Despite the fact that the Leningrad campaign did not officially end until the summer of 1944 when the Finns were pushed back to their 1940 border, there was jubilation in the city and across the USSR. In May 1945 Leningrad was proclaimed a Hero City, it was a title bought and paid for with the blood of its citizens and service personnel.

Soviet artillerymen haul a light gun undercover. *Maskirovka*, deception and masking intentions, played a large part in deceiving German intelligence as to the full scale of the forthcoming offensive. (Courtesy of the Central Museum of the Armed Forces Moscow via Nik Cornish)

During December 1943 III SS Panzer Corps launched a series of spoiling attacks aimed at disrupting preparations in the Oranienbaum bridgehead. They achieved little other than casualties, one of whom is being moved to the unit graveyard on the back of a 20mm flak vehicle. (Nik Cornish at Stavka)

(Above:) Many of the Panthers assigned to the Nordland Division were faulty and very unreliable. The most useful armoured fighting vehicles were the thirty or so StuG IIIs of III SS Panzer Corps. This Panther model D is heavily coated with *Zimmerit* anti-magnetic mine paste giving it some protection against Soviet tank-hunting teams. (Nik Cornish at Stavka)

To replace casualties reservists were brought up from the rear or pressed into service from partisan bands. Here one such group receives instruction in the inner workings of a Maxim M 1910 machine gun. (Courtesy of the Central Museum of the Armed Forces Moscow via Nik Cornish)

The last of the German rearguard in Novgorod. (Courtesyv of the Central Museum of the Armed Forces Moscow via Nik Cornish)

The remains of a StuG III and its crew. Organized in batteries of six vehicles each, they were effective tank destroyers. Three batteries were deployed in support of the battle groups holding the connection between Sixteenth and Eighteenth armies. (From the fonds of the RGAKFD at Krasnogorsk via Nik Cornish)

T-34s of Second Shock Army advance behind smoke with their supporting infantry close behind. This army's 204th Tank Regiment lost nineteen tanks in short order when it ran into an undiscovered minefield. (Courtesy of the Central Museum of the Armed Forces Moscow via Nik Cornish)

SS infantry pause for food. The grenadiers of the Nordland Division were mainly recruited from Denmark and Scandinavia. The division was sent to the Leningrad region in December 1943 from Yugoslavia, where they had cut their teeth fighting partisans. (Nik Cornish at Stavka)

Panthers of SS Panzer Battalion 11 Hermann von Salza, the armoured unit of Nordland, fall back towards Luga. Although suffering heavy casualties, Nordland was strong enough to repel a Soviet seaborne landing at Merekula during February. (Nik Cornish at Stavka)

Tigers of 502nd Heavy Tank Battalion negotiate part-thawed terrain. Fuel drums are being salvaged from the lorry. An experienced formation, it included as platoon commander Otto Carius who ended the war with a total of over 150 'kills'. The Tiger was not designed as an offensive tank but reflected the Germans' need for a defensive vehicle. (Nik Cornish at Stavka)

Kissing his mother goodbye. The Red Army conscripted all males in liberated areas as infantry replacements. Many had taken refuge in the vast forests and swamps only to re-emerge when the advance swept into their area. However, their lack of training contributed to the high casualty rate of the Soviets during this period. (Courtesy of the Central Museum of the Armed Forces Moscow via Nik Cornish)

A Soviet 122mm howitzer fires in support of XXX Guards Rifle Corps as it advances towards Krasnogvardeisk. Here the remnants of L Army Corps with the support of a Tiger platoon fought off early attacks until the town was liberated on 26 January. (Courtesy of the Central Museum of the Armed Forces Moscow via Nik Cornish)

Officers and men celebrate the link-up between Leningrad Front and the troops in the Oranienbaum bridgehead south of Ropsha. The men of Second Shock and Forty-Second armies joined forces at 21.00 hours on 19 January. (From the fonds of the RGAKFD at Krasnogorsk via Nik Cornish)

The German cemetery in suburban Ropsha. (From the fonds of the RGAKFD at Krasnogorsk via Nik Cornish)

A patrol from 378th Rifle Division reconnoitres open ground near Novgorod. The premature attack launched by this unit kick-started the advance on the city by Fifty-Ninth Army. (Courtesy of the Central Museum of the Armed Forces Moscow via Nik Cornish)

Dozens of small groups such as this one made their way back to the German lines. Running the gauntlet of partisans and Soviet cavalry was a risky business made more difficult by the possibility of being shot by their own side, hence the display of the swastika as these men approach safety. (Nik Cornish at Stavka)

Restoring rail and road communications behind the advancing troops was a vital task as the advance slowed due to lack of supplies. Although Fifty-Ninth Army reached and crossed the Luga River on 30 January, it was incapable of taking Luga itself. This would remain the front line until the summer offensive. (Courtesy of the Central Museum of the Armed Forces Moscow via Nik Cornish)

An Estonian SS infantryman takes his place in the trenches. From the middle of 1943 larger and larger numbers of Balts had joined the German forces. They enjoyed a well-deserved reputation as fine soldiers. (Nik Cornish at Stavka)

Seen here presenting a banner to a newly honoured Guard formation, Zhdanov announced the end of the siege on 27 January 1944 with the following words: 'In the course of today's fighting a task of historic importance has been achieved: the city of Leningrad has been completely freed from the enemy's blockade and the enemy's artillery bombardment.' (From the fonds of the RGAKFD at Krasnogorsk via Nik Cornish)

As dusk fell the city's inhabitants rejoiced, raising flags and letting off fireworks. In Moscow 324 guns fired 24 salvoes to celebrate the event. For others tea and cake were enough. (From the fonds of the RGAKFD at Krasnogorsk via Nik Cornish)